CHA

CHANCES

My Story of Love, Sex and a Second Chance

By Penny
with Andrew Crofts

RedDoor

Published by
RedDoor
www.reddoorpublishing.co.uk

© 2015 Penny

The right of Penny to be identified as author of this Work has been asserted by her in accordance with sections 77 and 78 of the Copyright, Designs and Patents Act 1988

Hardback ISBN 978-1-910453-00-1
Paperback ISBN 978-1-910453-01-8

All rights reserved. No part of this publication may be reproduced, stored in a retrieval system, copied in any form or by any means, electronic, mechanical, photocopying, recording or otherwise transmitted without written permission from the author
A CIP catalogue record for this book is available from the British Library

Neither the author nor the publisher can accept responsibility for, or shall be liable for, any accident, injury, loss or damage (including any consequential loss) that results from using the ideas, information, procedures or advice offered in this book.

Cover design: Sheer Design and Typesetting

Typesetting: typesetter.org.uk

Printed in the UK by CPI Group (UK), Crodon CR0 4YY

To my Mom and James's grandmother: two very extraordinary women, who both gave us great lessons in life. They are always in our hearts – until we meet again.

A NOTE FROM ANDREW CROFTS

Their enquiry stood out from the usual half dozen that came through that day. James emailed that he and his girlfriend lived in Switzerland and were looking for a ghostwriter to tell their love story. He warned that it would contain sexual elements that many would find shocking, but that there would be many lessons to be learnt from it.

Dear Mr Crofts, if possible, I think that meeting up with us, seeing who we are, hearing us out, would not be a waste of time.

He told me they would be in London the following weekend and would be staying at The Dorchester in Park Lane. Curiosity got the better of me. Since I was going to be in Mayfair anyway, interviewing an African leader whose memoir I was ghosting, I suggested I pop into The Dorchester once I was finished.

The African leader had a busier schedule than expected and finding myself free in the middle of the day I sent James a text. He invited me to join them for lunch at Zuma's, a famous Japanese restaurant in Knightsbridge. It seemed that fate was working to make this meeting both pleasant and convenient. Even if nothing came of the book it would be an interesting lunch and would pass the time until my African client was free once more.

The couple I found waiting for me at the bar with perfectly chilled glasses of white wine were nothing like I had expected. To start with they were both extremely good-looking, but there was not a hint of arrogance. They managed to be both reserved and charming at the same time, intent on making me feel comfortable in their company despite the very obvious fact that they were completely wrapped up in their adoration of one another.

Plate after plate of tiny, elegant delicacies were presented at the table by discreet waitresses and one chilled bottle of wine followed another as they slowly revealed their fable of true love.

It started with love at first sight when they were little more than children and was shattered a few years later by the realities of adult life and the expectations of their families. Just like Romeo and Juliet the young lovers were forced apart by circumstances but, unlike Shakespeare's star-crossed lovers, these two had been given a second chance and they had turned it into something magical and extraordinary.

By the time the espressos were being served I was hooked and had agreed to fly out to Switzerland the following weekend with a tape machine. That was the start of a journey deep into the lives of a couple who together have discovered some of the most profound secrets of happiness. What follows is Penny's telling of the story.

Andrew Crofts

PROLOGUE

'Penny! Penny! Penny!'

I jumped up and ran to the steering wheel, pushing James out of the way. Gas on and tribord gear down, with a mighty churning of water the boat started to move backwards, away from the three sailing boats we were about to hit broadside.

'Oh my God, Pen,' James's face was still drained of all colour, 'you are the best! I totally panicked. I'm so sorry... I saw the boats coming towards us, with the wind... Fuck!'

'No problem, Captain,' I grinned, feeling really good about myself. 'I taught you how to handle two motors, but wind is tricky.'

I couldn't get rid of the proud little smile I had on my face. I'd got my man's beautiful ten-metre motorboat out of the port while he was freaking out. How good did that feel? I would say that James loves his boat nearly as much as he loves me. We have both been boat freaks since we were kids but I will always tease him that he is just a 'lake mariner' and that I have a sea licence.

Once he had recovered from the shock and we were safely out on the lake, James took over the wheel again and I stretched out in the front with my book, totally naked apart from my G-string bathing suit. I was deep into my biography of Oona Chaplin and wasn't taking any notice of where we were heading. The boat is completely open with a comfortable zone in front to chill out and read and sunbathe. James and I prepare it every summer with such joy, bouncing around like kids. We fill up the fridge with some good Domaine d'Ott rosé wines and some whites. I have all my shampoos and cosmetics on board. Huge towels and deco cushions make it feel just like home.

The wind dropped as suddenly as it had arisen. The lake is so unpredictable, thirty minutes before we had the 'Penny, Penny' crisis and now it was as smooth and calm as a mirror. James lowered the anchor just off a beach and I started preparing the sushi we'd picked up on the way down to the port that morning. I took out a nice bottle of Pouilly Fumé from the fridge and prepared us a picnic in the front, spreading everything out on the towels before settling down to enjoy the view.

'What do you think is happening in those bushes?' I asked, leaning forward to try and get a better look at the beach, my bum in the air. 'Why do they keep going back and forth like that?'

'I don't know,' James replied, rummaging under the seat for a pair of binoculars.

'I think I might swim over and find out what's happening,' I said.

'You're not going into that forest,' he said. 'And keep your head down or they'll see we're watching.'

I ducked down and took the binoculars from him. Two people came out of the undergrowth together and sat opposite each other on the sand, both cross-legged.

'Honey,' I said, 'would you light me a cigarette, please?'

As I focused on the couple I saw they were both really fit men, obviously guys who spent a lot of time toning their bodies in the gym, a pair of Greek gods. Both of them were naked and both already had magnificent erections. I began to feel really hot. They leant towards each other, their lips meeting in a passionate French kiss. It was a beautiful scene with the clear green waters lapping between us, the white stones of the beach and the dark trees behind these two perfectly built men.

They started to masturbate each other as they continued to kiss and with the binoculars I could see every sun-kissed muscle moving in their fabulous arms and toned torsos.

'I'm not interested in watching this,' James said, turning away for a couple of seconds before his eyes were inevitably drawn back to the scene. For me, on the other hand, this scene was exciting – so illicit and so weird.

I took a long drag on my cigarette and continued to watch, staying as still as I could, like a hunter, crouched doggy style in wait for their prey. I could sense that James was looking at my ass in the G-string. I was now imagining the sort of sex these beautiful guys had been having together in the bushes and I needed to do something about the heat that was building inside me. James gently caressed my buttocks, his fingers lightly brushing between the cheeks and down over the lips of my pussy, making me tremble. A tiny moan of pleasure escaped me. I needed to have him in me as quickly as possible. It's not that gay sex interests me or that I would watch or enjoy it, but I had been taken by surprise and the forbidden feeling made it actually sexy, something that a hetero girl doesn't usually come across in daily life.

I moved closer to James and we started kissing passionately, our tongues entwining as we caressed one another's bodies, our skins heated and scented by the sun, melting together in a balm of oil and sun cream. All the time I was watching the two guys out of the corner of my eye, becoming more and more excited as I guided James's hand towards my pussy and then behind. I was so turned on I wanted him inside me in every way just like I imagined the guys I was watching. I guided his fingers there and he started massaging my anus softly and slowly, gently masturbating my clit at the same time, gradually making everything more ready and comfortable. Since anal sex needs to be as smooth as possible in order to make it the best possible experience, lubrication is a must. I had my little bag with sun creams in front and discreetly handed him a bottle of sun tan oil. He took some oil in his palm and continued to massage my bottom.

The scene on the beach, mingled with the scent of James's sun-warmed skin and the gentle caress of his fingers was so arousing my breathing was becoming heavy and my head was feeling light. I took his rigid dick in my fingers and guided the tip inside my ass. We paused for a moment, enjoying the sensation of us being locked together, and then he started moving gently, sliding further and further inside, filling me up until I told him to take me harder, turning my head to kiss him at the same time, hungry for his lips, for the taste of his tongue. It was as close as we could feel, as in love and together as possible, transforming us for a few moments into one body.

Afterwards we were both lying in the front of the boat, holding each other close in a mixture of lube, sweat and sun cream, still out of breath from our overwhelming orgasms, when I heard James's phone ringing and knew immediately what this ring-tone meant – Aaron was at a loose end; a sunny Saturday, wife abroad... that would add up to a bored Aaron phoning in search of something diverting.

James picked up the phone and I was only half listening as I lay in the warmth with my eyes shut. 'We're about forty minutes from Lugano,' he was saying, 'Where are you? We can come pick you up but just don't be late. No, I need to fuel up so come over to the port.'

'I hope he won't make us wait for an hour,' James muttered as he climbed back behind the wheel.

'You know he will,' I shrugged. 'He's always late. It's like he lives in his own time zone.' But then again, things could be worse. Here I am, lying in the sun, sipping my wine with the love of my life and no kids on the horizon. It's not like we're waiting outside a bus station or something.

For a second my thoughts returned to Hannah and I wondered if her Dad would at least take her to the pool while the weather was so great. My thoughts were interrupted by the thrilling throb of the engine being turned on.

'Penny,' James shouted over the roar, 'Can you check that the anchor comes up right and click the chain?'

'Sure, Captain.' Any excuse to get me bending over so he can check out my tanned ass while I'm taking care of our safety.

Once we were under way I went back to Oona and her amazingly crazy life with her weird genius of a husband. What a love story those two had. Real, real love. In the background I could hear Bonnie Taylor singing 'Total Eclipse of the Heart' and I could feel the waves beneath us and my skin continuing to tan while my head was lost in the book for the next forty minutes.

As we approached the port I pulled on a little tunic dress to ensure I didn't distract the young man who fuels up our boat.

'Five hundred and fifty-eight Swiss francs, please,' he said once the operation was complete. 'Do you need a receipt, Sir?'

I couldn't help laughing at the expression on James's face.

'The little pleasures of a day out on a boat,' I shrugged.

We still had to wait more than half an hour for Aaron. You either accept it or you get angry; I accept it, James has more difficulty. Aaron didn't even accelerate his steps when he saw us and knew we were waiting and that the engine was already idling. Eventually he hopped casually onto the back platform and I unattached the ropes while James pushed the gas a little.

'Hi guys! What's up?' Aaron grinned, always ready to jump into the moment. 'How cool is this to be on the boat with you two guys on such a beautiful day?'

'A glass of wine?' I asked, passing the one I had already filled.

As we cruised across the lake, sipping our gorgeous white wine, we all smiled simultaneously. 'Cheers!'

James was looking out for somewhere we wouldn't be overlooked. Now that the wind was down and the lake was calm, it was all much easier. By the time we found a nice, quiet spot and I'd done my ass bends again for the anchor procedure, we were already halfway through the second bottle of wine and a few minutes later I was opening the third one. I was bouncing around the boat topless, making sure everybody was comfortable and then the idea struck me.

'You up for Trivia, guys?' I asked.

I knew we had a set on the boat from last year. I heard an 'okay' from both of them at the same time and within a minute I'd set up the table, got another bottle in the ice and we were squabbling about the rules.

'The one who wins a little stone can point out the person who has to do a forfeit,' I suggested enthusiastically.

'No,' James shook his head, 'the one who answers and wins a stone can point out the one who wants...'

Aaron was also giving his input and all three of us were already tipsy enough to find even the arguing funny. We finally agreed on my rules – as if it would change anything. Every time one of us threw the dice our hearts were thumping and the one who was reading the question to the other would hold their breath, not knowing if they would be able to answer or not. We were having a blast, laughing out loud and making fun of each other over each question.

'You'll never get this one in a million years,' James said when it was our turn, laughing delightedly at my perceived ignorance before he even read the question out.

'Shoot,' I told him.

'Okay. What is the name of the tanker that sank off the coast of France in 1999, causing an environmental disaster?'

'Erika.'

'How the fuck did you know that?' he yelled, hurling the cards at me in a childish tantrum which he hoped I would think was self-mocking.

Taking my time to enjoy my chance to gloat, I decided to make James point out the one who would do the forfeit.

'Take off your pants Aaron,' he said. 'Quick! All naked, please! Quick, Quick, Quick!'

It took us another round before we were all naked, the three of us just sitting there, giggling, with far too much good wine in our heads. The next forfeit was on me.

Unfortunately I didn't know which guy had won a gold medal during an Olympic game – sport has never been my strength.

'Penny,' James announced. 'Please go on your knees and taste Aaron for three minutes.'

I rolled my eyes and gave him a look that warned; 'payback time very soon, Honey.'

It was getting hotter and hotter. We were all three of us aroused big time by then and our inhibitions were leaving us one by one.

'Stop!' James shouted. 'Time over!'

Aaron sat back, his tight dick pointing up to the sky. We continued playing another round until James was lying on the floor on his back with me sitting on him, riding him gently. We were kissing each other, existing in a bubble, our bodies hot with excitement.

The warm wind was gently blowing through my hair and the sun was going down as James lay down on the deck and I straddled him, bouncing up and down, letting him watch my breasts thrusting forward, knowing that he was enjoying the sight of my tanned body stretching up above him. Aaron was standing beside me, his erection right in front of my face. I parted my lips and allowed him to slide it into my mouth again. James was watching from below, his manhood buried deep inside me as I took his friend's dick in and out of my mouth, sometimes slow, sometimes faster and rougher, depending on the pounding rhythm that James was creating with his own thrusts.

Nervous that the vision was getting too hot to handle, James was beginning to worry that he might come too quickly. There were so many conflicting emotions for him;

feelings of awkwardness at having his loved one sucking dick in front of him mixed with the excitement of seeing her tits rising and falling to his rhythm. There was a cocktail of adrenalin, panic and a little jealousy – all adding to the huge excitement.

Deciding to cool things down for a moment James made a sign to Aaron to take his place and handed him a condom, which he slid on discreetly before I sat on him, moving slowly once he was inside me and waiting for James to guide me as to what was going to happen next. There was no kissing with Aaron. He and I don't kiss. Never. Ever.

As I took Aaron's manhood inside me James was sitting at Aaron's feet, like he was watching porn, watching my ass rising and falling, watching my pussy being stretched, listening to my moaning. I turned around to check that he was okay, as we always do at moments like that. He started touching my ass, and fondling my breasts from behind, knowing that would excite me as much as him. He touched the sensitive rim of my anus, murmuring how 'perfect and pink' it was, circling it, inserting one finger slowly after moistening it with his saliva. He could tell he was driving me crazy. At that moment he remembered the lube bottle and slid his finger out again.

'Please leave it in,' I whispered, 'I love it.'

But he needed both hands to put the lube on his fingers and his dick. He then inserted two fingers and I thought I was going to explode. He and Aaron exchanged looks because Aaron could feel what James was doing to me. I was so ready and he could sense it. James squeezed Aaron's legs together and straddled his calves, very gently pushing me back down so that my tits were pressing against Aaron's torso. I was going wild and stuck my bum in the air, riding

Aaron hard. James slowed our rhythm to a complete halt so he could adjust his dick at the level of my ass, enjoying watching what he was doing, savouring the moment as he penetrated me with his lubed dick. It was the fullest feeling that I had ever experienced. I had the man I loved in my ass and his best friend in my pussy. It was not an easy position for any of us but wow, once the motion started we were all going crazy with me sandwiched between them, coming inside my head so powerfully that both of them could feel it.

'You have two dicks inside you, Love,' James whispered in my ear, his chest pressing against my shoulder blades, and then he couldn't speak any more.

All three of us were moving in a coordinated rhythm, all of us now occupying the same bubble. Aaron was touching my breasts and my nipples while James was kissing my neck. I felt overwhelmed by sensations, free, in total control and fulfilled in every way. We all three came together.

'I guess we deserve a dive, guys,' I said once our cardiac rhythms had returned to something approaching normal.

We dove into the lake, all still naked, laughing, looking at each other without having to say anything. There were actually no words. Back on the boat with fresh glasses of wine, our bodies cooled down and loud music filled the air as we pulled up the anchor and cruised slowly in the late afternoon sun towards Lugano port, me and Aaron falling asleep in the front while James smoothly parked the boat.

Aaron, as always, had business to take care of that night and left us with a wave. 'Bye, guys! Always a pleasure being with you!'

James and I cleaned up the boat a little, throwing an embarrassing amount of empty bottles in the bin. We cleaned up the Trivia and made the place look civilised again.

We didn't need to worry about covering it. We knew it wasn't going to rain that night and since Hannah wasn't due back from her father's until the following evening we planned to go out on the lake again the next day.

I pulled on my white summer dress and my new Chanel flip-flops, which I had bought like a freak three days before, and we were ready to hit solid ground again. With a stupid smile on my face I walked towards the car on legs that felt like jelly, as if I had been on a rollercoaster all afternoon.

As we drove away James smiled. 'You just had a "DP", Moneypenny,' he said.

'I know,' I grinned back like a girl who had just been given the most forbidden treat in the world. 'I know.'

CHAPTER ONE

It was 1988 and I was fifteen when I first saw James sitting amongst his friends in the café in Lugano. It was a Wednesday afternoon when everyone was free to come out of school for a few hours.

I was wearing a thick, green velvet Alice Band, my hair scraped back into a tight ponytail, and I was feeling deeply alone and miserable in one of the most beautiful cities on Earth. He, on the other hand, even though he was only two years older than me, looked effortlessly comfortable and classy. He was dressed more like a grown man who had already found his style than a teenage boy, handsome in a well-cut pair of jeans, a pair of brown Westons and a turtleneck, like he didn't need to prove anything to anyone. I loved his hair. It was a bit long, but very well taken care of and so thick.

What hit me first was his presence in the hot, bustling room. It's always the same; his personality completely fills any space that surrounds him, drawing everyone towards him, deliberately pulling them in and charming them. Although he's not a tall man, or loud, he is also not the kind of person you could ever overlook, even in a room full of bigger or louder people.

He seemed completely at home sitting at an already crowded table in the noisy coffee shop area behind the bakery. The warm smell of bread and pastry mingled comfortingly with the aromas of hot chocolate, coffee and cigarette smoke. The group all looked so relaxed together, so at ease in the world despite their youth, jabbering away in a mixture of Italian and English. I didn't speak a word of either language and I felt horribly far from my home and from my friends. I wasn't in my place at all and felt very shy.

At the moment I walked through the archway that divided the bakery from the café I didn't feel like I had anyone in my life apart from my big sister, who I knew from bitter experience could not be relied on to be kind to me. I felt lonely and vulnerable, which made me more than willing to allow myself to be wrapped up in James's charisma. I couldn't understand why my parents, who I adored, had decided so suddenly to send me away to a new school in a country where I didn't speak any of the local languages. I felt betrayed by them and isolated from the friends I would normally have gone to for comfort at such a moment. I lowered my eyes as everyone stopped talking and turned to stare, wishing the floor would open up and swallow me. They were all looking at me, like, 'the sister has arrived!'

James looked so relaxed as he jumped to my rescue and introduced himself that I would never have guessed he too had been experiencing an unfamiliar feeling of tension as he waited for my arrival.

'It was as if I'd had a premonition that something extraordinary was about to happen to me,' he admitted later. 'Your sister had shown me your picture, so I knew you were going to be beautiful, but that didn't explain why my stomach was actually aching with anticipation as I waited for you to arrive. I'd never experienced nerves like that before, merely at the prospect of meeting someone new.'

Although I was very unsure of myself, I think I knew that I was pretty because I'd heard people saying so, although I was always quick to deny it. I felt awkward and shy when people complemented me, not wanting to attract attention. Other girls of my age dressed in much more feminine and fancy ways than me. I was happier hiding inside oversized pullovers and jackets. I would never wear tight shirts or things that would define and expose my shape. I didn't really feel comfortable in my body.

Even at seventeen James was a confident guy, but something inside him was telling him that the girl he was about to meet was going to be different. I would never have been able to guess that he was nervous from his demeanour but the moment our eyes met I felt a connection between us, unlike anything I had ever felt before. We looked at each other and it was like an explosion. Both of us knew that something huge had happened and that neither of us would ever be the same again.

I think maybe my sister wanted to introduce us because James was the only one in her group of friends who could speak German, although he was certainly not fluent. Everyone in the room was as friendly as they could be but the language barrier made any attempts at conversation clumsy and uncomfortable. There is an unspoken code amongst pupils in boarding schools like ours. We had all been sent away from home by our parents, even if some of us were acting like we didn't care, and that shared sense of rejection bonded us together regardless of language, but the instant connection that formed between James and me was something more, way, way more.

'You possessed a beauty that was in a different league to all the other girls in the room,' he told me later. 'Even though you were the youngest there. You seemed shy because you couldn't speak the language, but I could see an inner confidence which told me to ignore the fact that you were dressed like a little schoolgirl, because inside that shell there was already a real woman.'

I couldn't tear my eyes away from his as he pulled me into the group. I felt shock waves travelling through every muscle and nerve in my body and somehow I knew that he was feeling the same jolt of electricity.

It was obvious he liked to charm everyone he met. It was a challenge for him to make people like him and I could see he was switching it on as he welcomed me to the table, settling me down beside him amidst the crush of bodies and coats, making a fuss about my arrival, ordering me a coffee, making me feel at home and making me forget the knot of misery that had been so tight in my chest since I had arrived in this new city. It was such a relief to find someone I could speak to. I'm guessing that to the others he probably seemed like he was being overly attentive but I didn't care. I was basking in the warmth of his smile, unable to avert my eyes from his as he talked. It must have been obvious to everyone else in the room that some sort of explosive chemical reaction had happened between us but I didn't care and it didn't seem as if he did either. He certainly didn't act as if he cared about anyone else round that table apart from me.

My sister must have noticed that something was going on because she warned him not to touch her baby sister. He laughed disarmingly at the idea and assured her that he had no such intentions, but I hoped he was lying big time because I wanted him to want to touch me as much as I wanted to touch him, an urge that would only ever grow in intensity as the years passed.

I couldn't stop looking at his face, at his eyes, which were so full of life and mischief and seemed to be looking through mine into my soul, reading and understanding all my thoughts. Then there were his lips, the sexiest I had ever seen, full, generous and well shaped. I could see they were soft without even touching them. I noticed he had two little moles on top of his upper lip. As I watched him talking in the noisy café, frowning in my efforts to follow whatever he was saying when he wasn't translating for me, I stared at those beautiful lips, wanting to lose myself in them. The way he stared unrelentingly into my eyes whenever he spoke to me made my heartbeat quicken and my throat constrict until it became difficult to breathe.

When we parted for the first time an hour or so later he took my hand and I felt an intense electric charge pass between us, a feeling that would alternately taunt and delight me every hour of my life from then on. James is not very tall but he is well built. He's not like a bodybuilder but he is sporty, well muscled while still having this small, cute thing about him. He kissed my cheek more firmly than I was expecting, allowing me to breathe in the heady scent of his skin for the first time and feel its softness. His smell made me dizzy. Now I know that it doesn't matter what perfume or eau de toilette he wears because it's his actual skin that smells like heaven. At that moment all I knew was that I had never smelled anything so completely wonderful, not even when playing amongst the many perfume bottles on my mother's dressing table at home.

Memories such as that first meeting in the coffee shop are like islands of happiness in those miserable, lonely, teenage years. Whenever we could be together I was completely filled with joy, a feeling that would vanish dramatically as soon as we were forced to part. I clung to every moment I spent with him like a drowning man clings to a life raft. Everywhere I went around school and around town my eyes were always searching for him, desperate for even a distant glimpse.

My section of the school was separate from his and I would sneak out whenever I could to meet him and his friends at the coffee shop or the pizza place or to play billiards, but there seemed to be interminable periods in between each precious meeting when I would be consumed by depression and frustration and I always felt like an outsider when I was with the others in the group that surrounded him. Most of them were Jewish and the subject of my nationality came up often in their discussions, some of them saying that my father being the age he was must have been part of the Hitler Youth. I had no experience of knowing anyone from a Jewish background and didn't know how to react, so I would shrug and stay quiet. Perhaps they thought they were just teasing, but it made me feel even more isolated. James would always come ferociously to my defence if anyone ever said anything even remotely critical in his hearing, but still I knew what they were thinking.

My father was born in 1926 and to most kids of his age, as with most of the German population at the time, Hitler was still a hero because he was promising a better life and none of them knew what was really happening. All my father knew was that joining the Hitler Youth meant he could be part of a group, fly model planes and have fun. It was like one long summer camp, plus he would get nice clothes and shoes, which was important to a boy from a poor family. Boys that age know nothing of politics. His parents were typically Germanic in their ways, strict and traditional, and my grandfather was also in favour of the regime without having any idea what they were actually doing. My grandmother, who I never knew but I was often told I resembled, had some Jewish blood from a great, great grandfather, but that meant we were officially 'not Jewish', even though my father was constantly talking about what a great people the Jews were.

Once my father was sent to war the reality began to dawn on him and although he never spoke about it I know he had a bad time. I once found a box full of letters that his mother had sent him when he was on the frontline, which he had kept and treasured ever since. It was the first time I was actually able to picture him having to fight, when he would have been a boy no older than James was when I met him.

* * * * * *

James and I could never spend as much time together as we wanted. I always seemed to be waiting; waiting for his calls, waiting to be able to get out of school, waiting for him to come back from home at the weekends. We didn't have mobile phones then so we couldn't be in touch every moment of every day as we are now. I was living in a constant state of solitude, never knowing when I would see him again or how long we would have when we were next together.

His parents lived not far from the school in Lugano, in a big house overlooking the tranquil waters of the lake and mountains beyond, so he would go home at the weekends while I remained imprisoned in the school buildings, waiting for him to return. During those endless weekends

I would spend hours and hours alone, thinking about him seeing Carla, his 'official' girlfriend, the one who had met his family and knew that side of his life away from school. He had made no secret of Carla's existence, but he had not told me what his feelings were towards her, skirting round the subject and leaving me to fear the worst.

Every time I heard her name it would send a chill down my spine. If I passed the school phone booth and saw him inside talking to someone I would feel physically sick. I hated to hear him even pronouncing her name. He had no obligation to be faithful to me since we weren't in an official relationship so there was nothing I felt I could say. The link we had between us had never been spoken out loud, even though we both knew that it was there. Both of us were too shy, too self-conscious to put into words what we were feeling in our hearts.

I assumed that he must be in love with Carla, otherwise he would have given her up, and so I never asked because I didn't want to hear what might prove to be the painful truth. But every time I thought about them together it was like a knife in my heart. I knew that it was important to his family that he settled with a Jewish girl, and I knew Carla wasn't Jewish either, which re-enforced my belief that he must love her really badly if he was willing to defy his family's wishes.

During the schooldays however, we spent every possible minute that we could in one another's company. Without ever putting anything into words we had become soulmates.

'The hours that I managed to snatch with you in the school schedule,' James has told me since, 'were the best hours I had ever experienced. Whatever was between us was huge. You weren't like the other girls in your group. You had a power, an aura around you, something special that overwhelmed me.'

I had no idea I was having this effect on him, being too shy and too unsure of myself to ever feel 'at home' in my surroundings.

Although he never spoke about it, he was already worried about his relationship with Carla and the way he felt when we were together was making him even more aware that that relationship was not right. It had been a challenge to win her, but once he had succeeded in that goal and had won her away from her previous boyfriend, he discovered she had problems with depression. Sometimes for him the challenge of winning something is more important than the prize itself. Once he had won her, however, he then felt that he had a responsibility not to hurt her. He didn't know how to end the relationship kindly and so he let it drag on instead. We wanted to be together every moment of every day, but James couldn't see how to get out of the other relationship without causing Carla harm. He had allowed himself to be sucked into it and now he was stuck in something that was too serious and too heavy a responsibility for a young boy. He had a tendency of get sucked into relationships and to be unable to extricate himself and I held back from putting any extra pressures on him. Although the presence of Carla in his life was an agony for me, I didn't challenge him about her. I didn't want to spoil the little time we had together by becoming a 'crisis girlfriend'.

* * * * * *

Everyone at school knew that we were a couple, even though it was never spoken out loud. Both of us were possessive and jealous of one another, despite the ghost of this other relationship hovering unspoken between us. Everything felt different when we were together because our connection was so instant and so total. We were overwhelmed by our feelings for one another. But James couldn't express how he felt in words because he didn't know how to end the relationship at home and I couldn't speak freely because I didn't know his true feelings for her.

Sometimes he would deliberately commit minor crimes in school like turning up late for studies or smoking in the wrong areas, so that he would be punished and kept back at weekends. Then he didn't have to go home and we had another opportunity to spend time together, living totally in the moment.

My sister had an apartment in Lugano and she said I could sleep there at weekends, albeit on a mattress on the floor, whenever she was out of town with her boyfriend. I could hardly believe that she was being so generous, giving me a key with which I could escape from the school dormitory for at least a short time and which could open the doors to freedom for me just a crack. Of course, if she had known what plans were forming in my mind she would definitely not have given her permission so lightly. The flat was on the ground floor, a little outside the centre of town. My sister had made no effort at decorating it; such things were of no interest to her. She didn't even bother buying a sofa and she had the tiniest television. The overall effect was incredibly depressing for someone who often had to spend their weekends alone, staring at the television and imagining her boyfriend at home with another girl.

The first Saturday night when I was granted this privilege I went to a nightclub with James and a group of his friends. We danced and drank and laughed as we always did when we were together and on the way back home from the club he sat close to me in the taxi, his arm around me, his body heat against mine, his warm, wine-scented breath in my ear as he whispered.

'I'm going to sneak out of school once everyone has gone to bed and come to you at the apartment.'

'You wouldn't dare,' I said, wanting to taunt him into proving me wrong, knowing how hard he found it to turn down any challenge, my body yearning for him with an intensity I still wasn't old enough to fully understand.

'Do you want to bet?' he asked. 'I'll bet you a bottle of vodka that I do it. I'll take a cab and come and see you, I swear.'

'Okay,' I laughed because even then I loved to bet, but I wasn't sure that even he would be able to get out of the school, however determined he might be to win the wager. As the cab drove away he made me a sign through the window, showing me he'd 'be back'.

After the noise and the companionship of the club and the taxi ride the silence of the empty apartment rang in my ears as I closed the front door behind me. There was no chance I could possibly settle down to sleep if there was even the slightest hope he might come to me. I paced around the rooms, constantly going back to check how I looked in the mirror, changing the lights, tidying and tweaking my sister's few possessions to try and make the room look more attractive, hardly able to breathe with the anticipation. The minutes dragged past, making me doubt that he would come, making me wonder how I would be able to cope with the disappointment if he didn't, re-enforcing my determination to stay hopeful and pacing, pacing.

An hour after watching the taxi drive away I heard a knock on the shutters.

'It's me,' he whispered, 'let me in.'

'Gosh,' I couldn't stop myself from smiling. 'I can't believe you pulled this one off.'

As I opened the window for him my heart was thumping in my chest, my stomach tight with nerves. The intensity of the excitement as he stood before me took me by surprise, making me light-headed. Having been dancing like extroverts just an hour or two before we were both now overcome with shyness as he took me in his arms and kissed me. He gently undressed me, down to my white lacy bra and pants, caressing every inch of skin as it was revealed, cupping my pert young breasts in his palms.

'Your skin is so soft,' he whispered, 'it feels like it's going to melt.'

However young and gauche I must have seemed, I was not entirely innocent. I had already lost my virginity before coming to the school, although I had never had any regular boyfriend. We slid down together onto the mattress as if all our lives we had been waiting for this moment to arrive.

With his soft breath in my ear it was as if the rest of the world had disappeared and at that moment I would not have cared if it had. We existed in our own little space of perfect joy, just the two of us, completely comfortable together and overcome with mutual passion. The now familiar smell of his skin made me feel so safe. The best smell was on his chest, his perfect chest with the perfect amount of hair. Still today I often go in there and breathe in his smell. That's the place where I feel the safest in the world.

We were both so innocent but so relaxed together. He didn't know if I was a virgin or not at that stage and that made him gentle and loving. Everything between us that night was smooth; never a moment of awkwardness as we stroked and kissed each other like we had been lovers for years and already knew one another's bodies intimately, as if every force in the universe was conspiring to bring our bodies together.

Sliding my pants down, he felt my pussy for the first time as he parted my legs. I was already moist, as if my whole body was letting him know how much I wanted him, that I was ready for him. He slid his finger inside me, the soft walls contracting tightly around him, making me moan, my lips on his ear, my arms holding him tight. He lifted his head, wanting to be looking into my eyes the first time that he penetrated me so that we would be locked together, body and soul.

His penis fitted as perfectly inside me as every other part of his body fitted with mine. There was never a need to worry about finding a comfortable position because being with him felt wonderful in any position we were in. We fitted together like Lego, our bodies automatically moving to the same rhythm. Whenever we sleep together our bodies always remain entwined like pieces of a puzzle, never coming apart during the night.

We had no protection that first time because nothing had been pre-planned, but we didn't care and we certainly couldn't have interrupted the natural flow of our lovemaking when it all felt so right. We could not possibly have stopped because we were being swept along by a tidal wave of emotional and physical euphoria, taking a wild, reckless, wonderful leap into the unknown.

The next morning, however, reality had to be faced and I needed to go to the hospital for a 'morning after' pill. We were both stunned by our stupidity. James felt terrible, taking me in his arms, racked with guilt.

'I'm so sorry,' he said, 'I should have been careful.'

'It's okay,' I replied, trying not to show him how scared I was. 'I'll take a cab to the hospital. Don't worry.'

I knew James wanted to come with me but also that he had to go so I assured him it was fine and I summoned up the courage to make the trip alone. It was an awkward experience since I still didn't speak the local languages with anything approaching fluency. Almost paralysed by shyness I felt certain the doctors were judging me, but even in a moment as frightening and lonely as that I regretted nothing because all I wanted was to be with him again, to hold him in my arms, to feel him inside me, to never have to be apart from him again.

* * * * * *

'Are you okay?' he asked when he called from home later. I could tell from the sound of his voice that he was still feeling terrible guilt at leaving me to cope on my own.

'I'm fine,' I assured him, sitting alone in the dingy little apartment. 'Are you having a nice weekend?'

I was already counting the hours before I would be able to see him again. Having once tasted the wonder of each other's bodies we could hardly bear to be apart. We wanted to be kissing, touching, tasting each other at every opportunity. I ached for him to be caressing my buttocks and my breasts, kissing my neck and my face. I longed to devour him and for him to devour me. But such opportunities when you are in a boarding school are tantalisingly and frustratingly rare.

Whenever James could save up the money, and once I had turned sixteen, we would go to a cheap hotel for a couple of hours in the afternoon. It was very clinical and very sparse, but it was only six minutes' walk from school and had a bed, which was all we needed. The tension would build from the moment we set out with the intention of booking in, rising as James strode confidently up to the receptionist, laid down the necessary documentation and paid for the room, aware that she would know exactly why we were there and that we were 'rich kids' from the famous local school, wondering if she knew any of our teachers and whether she would give us away in a casual conversation one day. The fear of discovery added another level to the excitement and urgency of these trysts.

Taking the key and mounting the stairs would make us breathless with anticipation. By the time we were actually alone in the room with the door locked behind us, and able to undress each other without interruption, our hunger for one another had already reached a fever pitch. Every detail of those short afternoons is etched into my memory. The bra that I wore was like an elasticated T-shirt with a lacy finish, very basic but still so beautiful as he peeled it away from my breasts, lifting my slender arms above my head. I wanted to touch and kiss every inch of him and our youthful lovemaking would become a frenzy of lust. Whenever we plucked up the courage to linger we started to experiment with tasting and licking one another, him growing intimately familiar with my pussy, me with his beautifully smooth, capped penis, teasing and tempting one another for as long as we could.

Once our heads had cleared of lust and our muscles had relaxed, we would become nervous once more at the danger of being discovered, dressing quickly in order to hurry down to the pizza house to meet up with our waiting friends. Today, of course, we would take advantage of the luxury of being able to lie entwined in one another's arms, just breathing in one another's scents and talking, talking all the time, but then we were still kids, frightened of being caught out, frightened that our parents would be informed of what we were up to. Our hearts still thumping in our chests, we would stride purposefully back out through reception again, deliberately not catching the receptionist's eye, stifling our joyful, triumphant giggles. The fear added to the sense of exhilaration that being with James always gave me.

James's parents didn't give him that much spending money, so we couldn't book a room every day, but we would still snatch moments together wherever possible. The enforced waiting made every contact all the more exciting and caused us to yearn all the more desperately for one another's bodies, making it all the more electric every time our fingers or our lips could meet.

One of the places we made love was the toilet of the local mama-papa pizza restaurant, where we could often be found in the middle of the afternoon. I would nearly always pay for our pizzas since my parents were more generous with my allowance, maybe out of guilt for sending me away from home so brutally. We would put music on the old-fashioned jukebox, which was filled with Italian love songs that played on our young heartstrings and inflamed our appetites as we ate and talked and laughed and never took our gaze off one another until we simultaneously saw 'the look' in the other's eyes and could bear the separation no longer, urgently having to be in each others arms, panting, legs entwined in confined places, everything frantic and passionate, heady and over very quickly for both of us, always leaving us wanting more of each other's bodies and minds, wanting more time together, more experiences to share.

The first time it happened in the toilet at the pizza place was totally spontaneous. We were both using it at the same time and met at the basin outside the cubicles. I was washing my hands and there was no one else in sight. We exchanged the 'look', which we both by then recognised whenever we saw it in the other's eyes, and were immediately kissing, reeling into the cubicle together and slamming the door behind us as James pulled down my underwear and I ripped open his pants, lifting out his erection. I was already moist by that stage, already aroused and breathless at the expectation of being able to touch him and feel his hands and lips on me. Both of us nearly always reached a climax at the same moment in these hurried trysts, but we never cared if we didn't either, just laughing it off, knowing we would be doing it again at the first opportunity.

The next time we were in the restaurant with a group of friends when the urge overcame us. We left the table together, which added to the excitement and the tension and the need for speed. We were sure we could hear stifled laughter outside the cubicle and then someone knocked on the door, building the sense of urgency and the excitement to an even more exquisite pitch before we eventually returned to the table, blushing but proud.

There was an English-style pub in town that had a pool table and a huge square table which we would sit round with friends, all of us drinking pints of beer. One evening we were sitting there when I felt James take my hand under the table, guiding it into his lap where he had opened his zip, allowing me to feel the soft-skinned hardness of his erection as I gently played over it with my fingertips. He slid his fingers inside my pants, and I immediately became wet. Both of us were having trouble breathing because of the heat of our desires, being almost dizzy with passion, but all the time we were keeping our straight 'poker' faces so that none of our friends would know what was going on just inches away from them. We were living our own secret life in the middle of a noisy crowded room, just the two of us. The challenge of getting away with something right under people's noses was so exciting that the thought of it aroused me almost as much as the act itself. It was tantalisingly scary, not knowing if our friends had seen what was happening or not. It probably only lasted a few moments and I did not make him come under the table, simply indulging in a cute sexual moment with no goal in mind.

We became more and more daring in the places we would use to be together, always searching for empty rooms where we might be able to snatch a few minutes together, the danger of discovery heightening the excitement. One night in the school canteen James made a sign to me to get up and he would follow me out discreetly. I strolled outside and waited, trying to look casual and not attract anyone else's attention. Suddenly he was beside me, taking my breath away just by being there. He took me by the arm, guiding me through the cloisters.

'Come quickly,' he said.

We walked until we found an unlocked window, which was my English classroom. Glancing quickly around James prised it open and we jumped through, hearts crashing in our chests. Taking me in his arms he laid me gently down onto my back on the table in front of the teacher's desk. He started to caress me under my pullover, slowly stroking it upwards, kissing my flat young stomach, all very gentle. Without saying a word he pulled down my pants, opened his jeans and slid inside me. It was so forbidden and so exciting, knowing someone could walk in and catch us at any moment.

The excitement grew as we tore each other's clothes off, both hungry for the other's body and instantly aroused by everything the other did. Once it was all over we remained entwined for a few moments, giggling and panting happily, before hunting around in the dark for discarded clothes and socks and hurrying back outside to meet the others for a last cigarette. Next morning I was waiting at the door of the same classroom when he strolled past. Pausing, he kissed me on the cheek, holding his lips there for several seconds before moving them to my ear and whispering, 'Enjoy your English lesson.' He left without looking back and for the next hour I didn't hear a word the teacher said.

CHAPTER TWO

There is something that I need to explain if James's actions in the following few years are to make any sense to the reader at all. When he was fourteen, after his bar mitzvah, he travelled with his family to Israel, as he often did, but this time his father thought it was the moment for his eldest son to be taken to visit the famous Holocaust Museum in Jerusalem. Although James's grandparents had been forced to flee the Nazis and take refuge in Switzerland, it was not a subject that his father had talked to him about in any great detail. Despite the fact that it was fundamental to the way his father viewed himself, his family and the world, he did not want to burden James with the full horror of what their people had been through relatively recently until he felt the boy was old enough to cope with the emotional burden.

'It's not unusual for young Jewish boys to have these things explained to them when they are on the cusp of becoming adult men,' James explained to me. 'I was still just a kid and I had no idea how serious it was to him. I really didn't want to go with him that day, preferring to surf at the beach and hang out with some young, sexy girls I'd met, but he insisted.'

His father is not the kind of guy you say 'no' to if he asks you to do something, certainly not if you are a teenager.

James has taken me to the same museum three times since then and I don't think anything can prepare you for the shock of seeing those displays and reading the words that have been written on the walls, especially if you are Jewish and you are just fourteen years old. The moment you walk in through the calm, sandstone walls from the bright heat outside you are confronted with a barrage of black and white images of Hitler, the Nazis and the absolute horror of life in the concentration camps. The museum is designed to lead you through history past the flags of the Third Reich, flags bearing the Star of David, on and on past glass cases containing hundreds and hundreds of objects; shoes, clothes, suitcases, purses, toiletries... Everyday items that belonged to real people, who were taken to the camps, stripped of their possessions and dignity before being robbed of their lives. There are the toys of the murdered children, letters from families, clothes, spectacles and human hair. There is a cattle truck from one of the trains that brought the people to their deaths and one of the gas chambers where the journey ended for millions of them.

'The reality of the holocaust overwhelmed me in the few hours we spent there that day,' James told me. 'Everything I was seeing and hearing and learning tore at my heart as I realised the enormity of what my grandparents' generation had been put through. I had never given any thought to what had happened in those death camps, and I had never seen my father cry until that moment.

'The picture of Elie Wiesel, the political activist and Nobel Prize winner, sitting on his bunk-bed amongst so many people who did not survive has haunted me ever since, as has the sight of my father, who I had always known to be so strong, weeping as we left the building.

'I read the sentences that were printed up on the walls, explaining that everything I was seeing and feeling inside that building was the reason why Israel existed and at that moment those words became engraved in my soul.'

As the two of them drove back home, while the boy's emotions lay in shreds, James's father explained why he had taken him there that day.

'What you have seen,' he said, 'is what one man tried to do to erase the Jewish religion and the Jewish people. Would he have succeeded Israel would not exist. So, if you do not marry a Jewish girl you will be doing the same as him because there will be no prolongation of the Jewish heritage. That is why you have to marry a Jewish girl.'

'He spoke with such force,' James remembered, 'such certainty and such emotion that I could do nothing to protect myself from the words.'

He had been hanging out with many non-Jewish girls by then, including Carla, his first girlfriend back in Switzerland, but at that moment it seemed to him that he could not possibly disobey his father's instructions when the time came to choose the mother of his future children. By the time he met me a few years later his father's words had calcified in his brain, becoming a rock that could never be dislodged.

One Friday night James and I were at my sister's flat. We were cuddling and kissing and getting drunk on Ballantine's whisky on the rocks, listening to Italian love songs, ballads which still make the hairs stand up on the backs of our arms when we hear them more than twenty-five years later. James didn't technically have to go home because he was driving himself by then and he could have phoned and told his mother he would be back in the morning. But he knew that Carla was very depressed. As the evening wore on and we lay entwined together I asked him to stay, but he didn't. Many years later he told me that he cried all the way home in the car because he felt that his heart was being ripped in two and he didn't know what to do about it.

'I knew then,' he told me later, 'as I struggled to see the road ahead through my tears, that you had had some sort of profound influence on me, that you had marked me in some deep way.'

But still his father's words echoed in his brain, telling him that what he wanted most in the world was going to be impossible. By the time he reached home he couldn't bring himself to go and see Carla, feeling an overwhelming compulsion to ring me instead.

'I couldn't possibly have gone another moment without hearing your voice,' he said.

'So, why don't you come back?' I asked.

'I can't... I can't.'

We talked for hours that night, but still neither of us admitted the truth about how deep our feelings were for each other. I felt that he was as desolate to be apart from me as I was to be separated from him, but still we didn't put those feelings into words.

* * * * * *

No matter how much pain I felt, I never tried to force James to give up his relationship with Carla. I never went crazy at him. I always thought that if someone wanted to be with me they would do anything to make it happen. I would never beg or go running after a man, however much I might long to be with him. I guess that's why we never actually knew how much we loved one another.

James didn't dare tell me and I always thought he didn't really, really love me deep down so I didn't ask. On the other hand, when our bodies were close the feelings we experienced could only be described as love, likewise the feelings of complete pleasure we felt when we were in one another's company, constantly talking and constantly laughing. It's as if we always missed by a second the opportunity to tell each other the absolute truth about how we felt for fear of breaking the spell, of damaging something that was already perfect.

As well as being my soulmate, and the man I lusted after every moment of every day, he was also my absolute best friend. I knew I could never be the 'official girlfriend'. I could never be the one going on holidays with him and his parents. I was not part of that picture. I was a blonde German girl, whose family they did not know, tucked away in a boarding school, speaking a different language. It could not happen, but at the same time I could not envisage any sort of life without him and so I held out hope that things would work out in the end.

I did meet his parents and other members of his family, but always as part of a group consisting of two girls and five guys, never as a girlfriend. James promised that once he had finished all his exams he would invite me out to Israel to stay with his family when they were out there, and I chose to believe him, allowing myself to pin all my hopes on him keeping his promise.

* * * * * *

'You need to leave school and come home to look after your mother,' my father told me. 'She may die.'

We had all discovered that Mum had cancer during the winter holidays. She was only forty-nine years old and it seemed impossible that such a strong, vibrant woman could be laid so low so suddenly. We were already frightened and none of the doctors in Spain, where we now lived, were able to make us feel any better.

'I'm taking your mother out to America,' Dad had told us. 'That's where the best doctors are. She will be operated on there.'

Now she was back in Spain but she was still sick and about to start a course of chemotherapy, already weakened by losing a breast. They needed help because Dad was flying around on business the whole time, and I was the one best placed to go home since I still had two years before I had to sit my A-levels. It did not occur to me that there might be any alternative, it was simply what had to be done. Already distraught with worry about my mother, my heart was now breaking at the thought of having to leave James and the others at school. All around me my newly made friends were packing up their stuff, chattering happily at the thought of the coming holidays, laying plans for when they would meet up again the following term. I wandered around empty rooms, grateful for their big goodbyes and their tears as they hugged me, even though they only served to make me sadder. I couldn't stop crying, feeling so desperate and sad.

The worst part was imagining that James would be coming back to the school the following term and resuming his life there without me. The only hope I could cling to was that his promised invitation to Israel during the holidays would materialise and I would somehow become part of his life outside the school.

When I thought about the reality of going to Israel with his family I was excited by the prospect, but nervous at the same time. Would our relationship be as strong away from the private world we shared within the school? Would it survive the scrutiny and disapproval of his parents? I could only hope and dream that it would because if it didn't what hope was there for us? Deep down, I feared that it would never work out, that it was mere dreaming on my part, more hope than reality.

Each day I waited for the call to come from Israel, telling me to go to the airport. Each day I would phone the hotel where they were staying and I can still remember the voice of the woman who answered the phone and assured me she would pass on my messages. But the call never came and I eventually had to accept that the vacation was never going to happen. Trapped in the quiet of my mother's sick room I felt like I was drowning in loneliness, but in moments of complete honesty I had to admit that I was not surprised. In my heart I knew there was no future for me with James as far as his family was concerned. His parents had met when they were fourteen and had been together ever since, never looking at anyone else. That was the culture of the family. James was expected to find his Jewish wife as soon as his schooling was over, have children and stay with her until the end. He didn't stand a chance, sucked in by hundreds of years of tradition, culture, history and family expectations. His parents were already displeased that his first girlfriend wasn't Jewish; there was no hope that they would accept him moving on to a German girl like me, however much we might love each other. I knew all this, although I didn't necessarily understand it. And at the back of my mind lingered the thought that perhaps he didn't really feel the same way about me as I did about him anyway or he would have made the call regardless of the consequences within the family.

I knew that James would have no idea how much I was hurting that summer and how angry I was, but equally I didn't find out for many years how much he was yearning for me at the same time, thinking about me every hour of every day we were apart, just as I was thinking about him.

His confusion was as debilitating to him as my loneliness was to me. In amongst the chaos of his beliefs and emotions, however, there lay one fundamental certainty, that if he did not marry a Jewish woman any kids he had could not be Jewish and he would have played a role in eradicating his own people. His father's words from that day at the Holocaust Museum never stopped ringing in his conscience. How could he put his own personal gratification ahead of his duty as a Jew? The very idea was impossible for him to entertain.

James still had another year to go in the school but I had to accept that I was leaving him behind, just as I had managed to settle into the school, learn the languages and make friends. I had started to feel like I belonged and now I was back on the outside again. The summer ended and I could picture all too clearly what his life was like in Lugano, in the buzz of the coffee shop, the pizza restaurant and the pub, surrounded by the same friends, laughing and playing games, drinking and dancing in clubs, while I stayed at home with my poor, frail mother, a woman who had once been so strong and beautiful and vibrant and had been such an inspiration to me as a child and who now felt ill all the time and had to wear a wig to cover her hair loss.

Living more or less alone in the big house in Spain as winter descended dragged my spirits even further down. Everywhere was closed up for the season and there was nowhere for a young girl to go and nothing for me to do in order to take my mind off James and everything he might be doing without me. It was like being locked in a gigantic golden cage and my longings grew to be physically painful.

The thought of living my whole life without him was almost too agonising to bear, but I knew there was no chance that he would choose to be with me once he left school and started making all the adult choices that his parents insisted on. Still I couldn't find the words to tell him how I felt, or maybe I instinctively didn't want to back him into a corner when I knew how painful it was for him as well. Sometimes I thought perhaps it would all work out in the long run if I was just patient. If we were meant to be together it would happen. At other times I didn't think I could endure the agony of waiting silently any longer and I would want to end the relationship once and for all, lashing out in an attempt to make the pain in my heart go away, but the pain of cutting the last of the ties would have been unbearable and so I kept clinging on to the last shreds of hope.

At weekends, when my father came back home to take over the nursing duties, I would get on a plane to Lugano and go looking for James, pretending to myself and everyone else that I just wanted to hang out with him as a friend. I wouldn't tell him how unhappy I was, how trapped I felt at home because I didn't want to spoil the little time that we were able to be together. We would just concentrate on partying and having as much fun as possible in the few hours that we were able to snatch. He never talked about how he felt either, that would have been like deliberately walking into a minefield, so I had no idea if he felt the same way I did.

I tried starting other relationships but they were merely pale imitations of the overwhelming feelings I had for James. I always found myself thinking about him when I lay in bed, imagining him with me whenever I was alone, picturing him naked and wanting them to be his fingers playing between my legs, rather than my own or some other boy's. The memories of him would make me moan with pleasure until the moment when I came and it was all over. At those moments I would feel even more alone.

Even as we saw less of each other I still went back to Lugano regularly to see my friends. It is a small place and whenever I was in town I would inevitably end up in the same nightclub as James. One night I went in with some friends, secretly hoping as always that we would bump into him, and my heart gave a familiar lurch when I saw him sitting with a woman in a dark corner of the room. The woman had dark hair and looked like she might be from somewhere like South America. She was wearing an ugly red and pink tailored skirt and jacket, the sort of thing a middle-aged woman might wear. Seeing him with someone else gave me a physical pain in my chest, accompanied by the heart palpitations that always happen when I see him.

'That's his fiancé,' someone said when they saw me looking over. 'They just took a flat together.'

It was like I had been punched in the face. I reeled back from the shock. The words were so final, so absolute, as if I had to give up every last shred of hope that I had been clinging to that I would ever be happy. I was in shock, uncertain what was happening until I found myself locked inside the ladies' bathroom with tears streaking through my make-up. I wanted to faint, to escape from the pain and the misery, but I didn't. There was no escaping it. I forced myself to breathe deeply, to keep going. Even when I found the strength to stumble back into the club in a trance, I wasn't able to speak to him. He didn't try to speak to me either. I think he felt ashamed and embarrassed. All night I just stared with blank eyes at their table, and drank far too much. At one point I saw her leaving the table and going to the bathroom and I got up to follow her, wanting to see her close to. I stood next to her at the basins, washing my hands and trying to figure out how she looked and how she smelled. I couldn't understand what he could possibly see in her. I tried to picture them being intimate and it made me feel nauseous. It was like my whole body had been poisoned.

* * * * * *

But still I couldn't think of losing my best friend and it wasn't long before I had engineered an introduction to James's fiancée through friends and found out everything I could about this woman who was going to be given everything that I wanted. Her name was Cecilia and I could see that she was exactly the sort of girl that his parents would be happy for him to marry; the one they would want to be the mother of his children. No job, no real degrees, the perfect housewife and future mother and, of course, Jewish.

I couldn't understand what James saw in her as a person, and in a way I found some comfort in that. Surely he must simply be marrying her because she was 'suitable' and if that was the case, what were the chances of the marriage lasting, especially as he was still only twenty-two years old? She certainly wasn't ugly, but she certainly wasn't pretty either. She was thin, but her body was nothing special. She was always talking, even when she had nothing to say. She seemed fake, pretending to be the nicest person in the world when in fact she turned out to be one of the most unpleasant people I had ever met, always late and pretending to be busy but never actually doing anything. She wasn't good news and I could sense that this wasn't going to be good for James.

I was devastated by her arrival on the scene, but then I had already been resigned to the fact that James was not attainable for me, and I was experienced at handling sadness. The fact that I had been unhappy for so long made me able to accept the news with stoicism once I had got over the shock, even though my heart was breaking all over again.

CHAPTER THREE

My mother didn't die and as soon as she was better I was able to escape from my deadly life in Spain. I moved back to Lugano permanently to study catering and set out on a career that would make me independent of my family. I chose Lugano because I knew it and had friends there, and because I still couldn't resist the temptation to be close to James, even though the logical part of my brain did not believe that anything would now change in his situation. He was still the best friend I had ever had. I knew that he would go ahead with the marriage now that he was committed because he always honoured his commitments but I hoped that we would at least be able to enjoy some time together as friends. I made a special effort to be friends with Cecilia, even though she was not the sort of woman I would normally have had as a friend, so that she would invite me into their lives and allow me to be around him.

I knew that in many ways this was making things worse for me, that I might recover more quickly from my broken heart if I started again somewhere else, but I wasn't ready to have him out of my life completely. I couldn't work out if I was unhappier when he was nowhere in my life, or when I got to see him regularly, knowing all the time that we could not be completely together, that he now 'belonged' to another. I was being ripped in two but I tried not to talk about anything negative when I was with him, wanting every moment we had together to be as happy and perfect as possible. Part of me wanted to run a thousand miles away from the situation which was causing me such misery, but a stronger part still wanted to be close to him, no matter how intense the pain might be.

My sister was also living in Lugano and she had also become good friends with Cecilia. I found myself being drawn into James's social circle by both of them. I even joined in with the plans for organising their giant, elaborate wedding. It was so accepted by the group that we were best friends that I was going to be sitting at James's table at the reception. My brain was on automatic pilot, not wanting to think too much for fear that I would see clearly the suffering that the future now inevitably held for me. Even during these moments of torture I still preferred being there to the option of no longer being part of James's life at all. To walk away from him completely still seemed like an impossible thing to do, a pain too unbearable to even contemplate.

The situation had evolved over such a long time it almost seemed inevitable and bearable. Almost. When James and I were together we were still soulmates, but now we could not touch for fear of where it would lead us. If our hands accidentally brushed we would jump apart as if we had been electrocuted, but we couldn't possibly do anything about it. If we had started to kiss we would never have been able to stop.

I would remember how it had felt when we had sat beside each other in the pub at school and he had unzipped his pants, taking my hand and placing it on his erection while he slid his own fingers up between my thighs, under my skirt, inside me, both of us so excited under the table with our poker faces to the world above. Now we were using our poker faces again to cover up the turmoil we were enduring internally, but we were no longer pleasuring one another under any tables and the fact that we could no longer touch one another increased the heat of the atmosphere between us, turned a screw on the pain of frustration, increasing my heartbeat whenever I was near him, making it hard to breathe.

There wasn't a moment when I didn't long to be touching him, but I knew he would never do anything inappropriate with me now that he was engaged. He would peck me on the cheek, as a friend greeting a friend, filling my head with his scent and reminding me how wonderful his skin felt against mine, making me long to feel his lips on mine.

'It wasn't so much that I was being loyal to Cecilia by not trying to touch you,' he explained to me later, 'it was more that I would never have been willing to demean you by making you my mistress now that there seemed no hope I could ever make you my permanent partner. I respected you far too much to do that.'

I kept trying to start relationships with other men, partly because I could see there was now no future for James and me, and each time I did so I would make sure he knew about it, hoping that I might be able to make him jealous enough to declare his love for me and call off his marriage in the sort of vast romantic gesture you might see in the movies, all the time knowing in my heart that this was real life, not the movies. James was the love of my life and sometimes I wondered if I was the love of his. Now I know that his agony was as great as mine, but then he hid it bravely, even from me. He knew that he was marrying the wrong woman, but for his family she was the right woman and that was the greater duty as far as he was concerned.

* * * * * *

Cecilia didn't appear to want to spend any more time with James than she had to, whereas he and I still wanted to share everything. Whenever any tiny thing happened to him it was me he would ring to tell, me he wanted to talk to about it, knowing that I would share his excitement or his laughter. It seemed like it was me he wanted to share his life with, even though he was pledging to marry and have children with her. Since Cecilia never appeared to want to be alone with him she would be happy if I was there too. Perhaps they had nothing to talk about when they were alone, or perhaps having a third person there stopped them fighting all the time. Whatever the reason she never made me feel that I was intruding on their relationship, never made me feel unwelcome. It was hard to work out what she thought of me.

Although I loved being with him, every dinner or lunch was an ecstatic agony. I longed to see him whenever we were apart, but when we were together I longed to touch him and to have him touch me. So often we would be sitting opposite one another across a table and there would be electricity in the air. Anyone else who was in the room with us must have known how we felt about each other, even when we weren't certain ourselves, but Cecilia seemed oblivious as she chattered on.

Whenever she said something foolish, which was most of the time, James and I would catch one another's eyes; both of us knowing exactly what the other was thinking.

James wanted to talk about his career plans, but Cecelia was not interested in the details, only the money that he would one day be earning and the plans she had for spending it. She thought he already had huge money but that wasn't the case. At that stage he was not being paid much, although he was showing a lot of promise, and was still having a lot of things subsidised by his father. He was highly motivated, ambitious and smart but he was still on his first job and not earning anything like enough to match Cecilia's spending ambitions. She was too wrapped up in the ring and the wedding arrangements and planning exactly when they would start having children to notice anything that might be happening around her. She was already mapping out their entire future, while I had no real plans, just wanting to dream and have fun, excitement and love.

I don't know how, but I found myself completely pulled into their wedding plans and organisations. Cecilia wanted the big Jewish wedding as much as both sets of parents did. James's parents wanted to be able to invite business contacts as well. There were going to be four hundred guests, most of whom James didn't even know. How weird was that? I was helping to organise my biggest love's wedding to a complete bitch, who I couldn't stand. I willingly allowed myself to be sucked into it and I guess James was happy to have me around as things got more and more complicated. The day Cecilia showed me two pictures of the dresses she was choosing between, I pointed out the less sexy one, of course. What else would any girl do? Perhaps I was in a dream world during those months, maybe fantasising that it was going to be me instead of her who would walk down the aisle in that white dress. As far as James was concerned, he couldn't have cared less about the details of the arrangements and could not give a fuck if the candles were green and the flowers white. He was far too overwhelmed by the immensity of what was actually happening to his entire life.

'Take the blue Villeroy & Boch ones,' I said as we stood staring at the displays in the wedding list shop while Cecilia busied herself at another counter.

'Isn't this ironic, Pen?' he said, looking up into my eyes. 'You're choosing our porcelain.'

It certainly was ironic – and heart-breaking too.

On the way to his wedding, sitting in the car with his best man, James kept going on about how worried he was for me and whether I was going to be all right. He had poured his heart out already and, unknown to me, his friend had tried to persuade him to cancel the wedding and go with me instead.

'Phone her,' his best man said as they drove on through the mountains towards the wedding, where we were all waiting for his arrival. James didn't need telling twice.

'Penny,' he said as soon as I picked up. 'I'm not sure I'm doing the right thing here...' He tried to defuse this bombshell with a shy laugh.

'Don't worry,' I heard myself saying, without knowing why, my heart thumping in my ears. 'It's not over between us. We'll be together one day, eventually.'

* * * * * *

Our beautiful, agonising friendship continued all through the horror of the wedding. Don't get me wrong, it was a beautiful wedding, with lasers and a band and everything you would expect for such a grand family celebration, but having to watch him marrying another woman was like a slow death. Despite my unhappiness at the way my own life was going, and my desperation to be with him, I was strangely unworried about the long-term future. Because Cecilia was such an unsuitable match for him the whole thing seemed to me to be a sham, doomed to fail sooner or later. I knew he didn't love her. If I had thought he did I wouldn't have been able to be there or to see them together. When he phoned from the car, already on his way to the place where four hundred people were waiting to see him walk down the aisle, there was nothing I could do to change things. This wasn't a movie. We weren't going to be able to run away together with him still in his wedding suit. I had no option other than to be stoic and try to calm his fears, as a best friend should do.

Nothing really changed in our relationship after the wedding. I was still the 'close friend of the family' and I was also the first person James phoned on the day that his first son, Isaac, was born in the early hours of the morning. We had been having dinner the night before, all together in a Japanese restaurant, but still it was a terrible shock to hear that there was actually a child in the world who confirmed that James and I were not a couple in any way. I felt a surge of excitement for him as a friend, but at the same time my heart felt as if it would break beneath the agony of him fathering a child with someone else. Cecilia had been horrible all through the pregnancy and a pain in the ass. I could see that James was terrified of upsetting her.

I had watched as a friend as they moved into their first flat together and now I raised a glass with everyone else to celebrate when they had their first child, the first grandchild of the family, the first child amongst any of our friends. We both pretended that this made everything okay, but the pain inside me grew worse as the months passed and I could still never be sure how he felt about me, about her, about anything. None of it made sense, but it was a fact, Isaac was there and there was nothing we could do about it now. I assumed this was what being grown up was all about, unhappiness and disappointment and a frustration so deep and sharp it was arousing.

I went over with a gift for Isaac and, despite the pain, I kept going round to visit them. The agony of our longing for one another was growing to levels which both of us could sense were dangerous. Cecilia would go off to the bedroom to breastfeed for hours, leaving us alone in the salon, unable to talk freely and unable to put on the television or music as a distraction from our pain because everything in the house had to be quiet for the baby. We could hear the gurgling sounds from upstairs through the baby alarm, intensifying the tension between us.

We never put it into words, but we both knew what was on our minds. The heat between us was palpable; we could not stop staring into each other's eyes. It was impossible to tear my gaze away from his perfect face, watching all the tiny expressions that I knew so well, remembering all the times I had stroked and kissed him, felt his lips on mine, our tongues entwined; the sweet taste of him... and now we had to sit between silence and awkward, foolish small talk. They were the longest hours of my life, but I didn't want them to end because they would only end once I had left the house and I never wanted to go. I never wanted to be apart from him for even a minute. The strain was becoming impossible to bear.

James was always making excuses to get out of the house, telling Cecilia he was going for videos or cigarettes. I was living only six or seven minutes' drive away and he would be on the phone to me from the moment he stepped out of the door, just to hear my voice, just to chat.

He never criticised Cecilia to me, he was honourable like that, but even when we were making each other laugh I could hear the unhappiness in his voice. I felt so sorry for him because I could see how unstable and abusive she was and I could understand why he would now have to stay with her in order to bring at least some stability into Isaac's life. There was just no point of connection between them as a couple but they were now tied together forever as parents.

One time he bought Cecilia a fabulous car as a surprise gift and he was so thrilled he called me to come and see it, to be there when he gave it to her. I was as excited as he was but when she saw it she just said, 'Why didn't you get it in black?' He looked so deflated I wanted to take him in my arms and make all the pain disappear but I had to stand and watch as she walked away to deal with the needs of the child once more, leaving us both standing, looking at each other, both wanting to get into the car and drive off together. But of course I had to go home and he had to go back into the house alone.

I knew how he was suffering, but still I did not know how he truly felt about me. I knew I was his friend and I knew that he lusted after me in a way he certainly didn't lust after her, but would that ever be enough to overcome all the guilt and conditioning of generations before him? I didn't think so.

Not wanting to accept that I might never find anyone else to love, I was trying to make a relationship work with another man, but still I would talk for as long as James wanted whenever he called, unable to resist picking up, unable to say no, unable to hang up on him. It was all such a mess, there was no hope and unless I wanted it to continue like this for the rest of our lives I had to stop it.

CHAPTER FOUR

'I don't want you to phone me any more,' I said.

I was talking on my first cell phone as I drove my car, during one of our countless conversations, about two months after Isaac was born. My words shocked both of us, feeling like I was pushing a knife into both our hearts. I could hear no sound at the other end of the line and I instantly wanted to take my words back, but I knew I couldn't.

'Penny,' he said eventually, 'you can't do that to me. You are my only breath of fresh air. How can you forbid me from phoning you?'

'It doesn't make sense, James. You have your son, you are more than double screwed in your marriage and I deeply pity you, but I can't go on like this.'

I could hear the sadness in his breathing and it was an agonising hang up. That was it. It was done and over. I was so angry and upset to have got into such a shit situation with nothing for me at the end of it. To me it seemed that Cecilia had it all, even though I wasn't even close to being in the mood for having babies of my own.

On the day of his wedding I'd told him it 'wasn't over' between us. It still felt like that, although I couldn't have explained why since I could not see any logical way in which we could be together. I knew he wouldn't leave Cecilia with a young child and I feared that if we kept going the way we were we would inevitably start having an affair and I didn't want that. It wasn't what we were about. There was always the possibility that perhaps I had been wrong to say that it wasn't over. Perhaps I had to face it. Perhaps it was over and I needed to move on or else I would just shrivel up and die. Not having him in my life still seemed like it would be too painful to bear, but the prospect of continuing like this had finally grown to be worse. I had run out of options, run out of hope. I needed to protect myself.

When I told him that the phone calls had to stop, that our friendship had to end, James knew I was right, but I could tell he was as horrified by the prospect as I was, feeling that we were finally saying goodbye to our last hope of happiness. He had been clinging to the straw which I'd held out when he was so frantic with worry in the wedding car, but now it seemed that had been a fantasy we had both been relying on, now there was nothing to hang on to apart from the reality of our unhappiness. As I ended that call I felt like my life was over, even though I knew I was going to have to find a way to keep going from day to day.

Not a day went past after that when I didn't think about James and our relationship and how we had somehow let something extraordinary slip away from us, something that would have been so wonderful had been replaced by things that were so dreary and ordinary. Not a day went past when I wouldn't masturbate with him in mind, memories of our times together filling my head, leaving no room for the reality to seep in as I fondled and caressed myself to a climax. It didn't matter how much sex I was getting with other partners, I always longed to get back to the privacy of my thoughts of James, wanting to be alone with my memories and my fantasies, safe with the one person in the world I had felt totally comfortable with and totally stimulated by, always wondering if it was the same for him, wondering if this was what my life was always going to be like. It seemed like our relationship was something that was still waiting to happen, and yet now we were set on two different courses that would probably keep us apart to the ends of our lives.

I can remember nearly every place that I was when these thoughts would attack most vehemently. I might be sitting at some traffic lights, or in a bar, or at home in the kitchen and the thoughts of him would flood into my head, his absence overwhelming me.

Sometimes I would see him passing in the distance, just one more person in the crowd, so familiar and yet so far away and untouchable, and my heart would start to thump uncontrollably. If I was in a car I would have to keep driving but it was like I was on automatic pilot as I fought to regain control of my senses and my body, to calm the banging in my chest, slow the pumping of my blood and cool the sweat that sprang to the surface of my skin, making me prickle with a hopeless sense of longing. I spotted him a couple of times in a restaurant and sometimes I just saw his car speeding past and knew that he was inside, carrying on his life without me.

I had a few boyfriends, but nothing serious, concentrating more on my career. I had a job as a consultant in the hotel business, which allowed me to travel all over the world and meet lots of men. They were not healthy relationships, partly because I was so messed up inside my head, however in control I might have appeared in my working life. Then I met Frederic, who I liked enough to move in with. I kept hoping that I would meet someone else who would have the same effect on me as James did, but it never happened and all my friends were ringing to tell me they were getting married and getting pregnant. It seemed that the choice for me was either to spend my life alone, living on my memories of those few wonderful years we had known each other and when everything had seemed possible, or I had to compromise and get on with life like everyone else seemed to be doing.

I heard that Cecilia had had twin girls, Rachel and Claudia, in a call from a mutual friend. I was alone in a hotel room in Singapore at the time and I had to pretend that it was no more than an interesting piece of news, when inside my whole body felt like it was being twisted and wrung out like a wet towel. When the call was over and I was alone in the silence of the anonymous hotel bedroom it felt as if nothing had changed and I would never be able to escape the pain.

* * * * * *

'I hear your great love is getting married,' Cecilia informed James when she heard the news. Apparently she always talked about me like that, in a flippant way, as if hinting that she knew the truth of our feelings towards each other and wanted him to know that it was of no importance to her. Did she keep me around her all that time in order to keep a watch on James and me? If she knew how he felt, how could she accept having me around at all?

'I put on my poker face when she gave me the news,' he admitted to me later, 'but I was falling to pieces inside. It was the worst possible disaster for me, as if all hope of ever escaping the hell I was living through had been eradicated in one blow. The thought of you being married to another man was so painful.'

I was happy to be marrying Frederic. We invited a couple of hundred guests to a Finca in Spain but I didn't invite James and Cecilia. I was determined to get on with my life and I couldn't have trusted myself to commit my life to Frederic in front of a crowd that contained James's face, feeling his sad eyes on me. I found great joy in finally organising my own wedding, just like any young girl fulfilling a dream. It was finally time to put the past behind me and move on with my life, throwing myself into the planning of the dress and the invitations and all that goes with them.

I made lists and had long discussions with my parents and my first arguments with my future husband about things like dress codes and whether babies should be allowed at the dinner party or not. I wanted to get both families involved, even though my dad didn't interfere much, trusting me with things like the negotiating of prices. I wanted a fun party and good food, rather than champagne fountains and fireworks. I wanted to handle everything myself, in my own way, which I did very well. It was like my first baby and I really didn't want any interference from Frederic's family.

The Finca was next to my parents' place and I arrived four days prior to the ceremony to ensure everything could be perfect on the big day – if only our relationship had been working out as well as the party arrangements. The whole thing seemed perfect although if anyone asked me to have a wedding like it now I would run a mile. In retrospect the whole thing seems like a ridiculous sham.

I chose my dress alone, not wanting to go with girlfriends, having a very clear idea in my head of the sort of thing I wanted. My mother wasn't the kind to get excited about these kinds of things either, and she wasn't really well during this period anyway. My parents never had a big wedding, they just ran to the City Hall between two meetings. They never consecrated it in a church and my mother never wore a white dress, but they married in 1963 and they are still together. My father had been married before for ten years and had a child from that marriage. It was still unusual to get divorced in the 60s. He had done all that white dress bullshit once and didn't think that it was necessary to do it again. He feels uncomfortable with priests and was already concerned that the whole church thing was going to last too long. He came up to fetch me from my suite at the Finca and saw me in my veil.

'Are you keeping that ridiculous thing on?' he asked.

'Yes, Dad,' I laughed, looping my arm through his as went downstairs. We walked through the lobby alone to the waiting limo.

'Sir,' he said to the driver as we climbed in, 'take the country roads please, not the highway. I want my daughter to have another fifteen minutes to think about what she's doing.'

Once we were on our way he turned to me. 'Honey,' he said, 'you still have time to change your mind. Just give me a sign and we can screw the church and drive off to a bar and have a great bottle of wine instead.'

I smiled. 'Thanks Dad, but it's okay. I know what I'm doing.'

Oh my God, I wish I had taken that opportunity he offered. But if I had would everything have turned out the way it has? All I know is that what my dad said to me that day was immense. It still warms my heart to think of those words. It proves to me just how close my relationship is with him and how much I have always been able to trust him. I was naive and blind and I know that I will be the same with Hannah, giving her every opportunity to run off if she so chooses.

We continued on our drive to the church and the party was great. The guests had fun and the flowers were as white as at any other stupid wedding. We got stupid presents and as stupid as I was I thought that that was all I needed to do to guarantee my future happiness; the ring, the dress, the pictures, the name... But it doesn't mean anything at all and it doesn't lead to a healthy relationship. I so much wish that the cash we spent on that stupid day was still in my bank account today so that I could use it for my daughter's school fees instead.

CHAPTER FIVE

Although I didn't know it at the time, when Frederic married me he was under the impression I had enough family money to set him up in business. I did not and so we both had to continue to work to support ourselves. He worked nights and I worked during the day at a variety of consultancy jobs. As a result we hardly ever spent any time together during the week and at the weekends he was always asleep and I was tiptoeing around him, not wanting to wake him up. Most of the time when I wasn't working I was at home alone, watching romantic movies on television, wanting to scream with the boredom and the lack of hope that anything would ever change, thinking all the time of James and the joy that we had always found in one another's company.

Our situation had a different effect on James, making him completely unable to watch the sorts of sad, romantic movies that I took refuge in, finding the pain too hard to take.

'The moment there was an emotional scene,' he told me later, 'I would start to cry and have to leave the room.'

They still break his heart today because he knows he should never have let me go, that he should have listened to his best man and told the driver to turn the wedding car around and drive in the opposite direction. Even today it's not possible to chill out with him and watch a romance.

Even *The Good Life* can make him emotional, causing him to jump out of bed and leave the room.

'Maybe I should make you watch the Teletubbies,' I tease him, 'Or Dora the Explorer.'

He feels he lacked the courage to follow his heart, but he is being too hard on himself because life is not a romantic movie. He allowed himself to be drawn in by other people's expectations of how his life should be. I don't think he will ever forgive himself for that one act of weakness and he blames his father for sowing the seeds of that weakness in his mind with his words and his tears. He was still only twenty-two years old when he made the decision to marry the wrong person, but he does not believe that's a good enough excuse to allow him to forgive himself for what he sees as cowardice. Like me, all through our time apart he was constantly masturbating to thoughts and memories and pictures of us together. Both of us were trapped on different sides of town, trying to lose ourselves in memories of one another.

'I couldn't get enough of you,' he told me later, 'even when you were no longer in my life. I couldn't stop myself from thinking about you all the time, wondering where you were and what you were doing. My eyes would be searching every crowded restaurant I entered, scouring every street I drove down, like a parched man permanently in search of a life-saving sip of water, even though he knows it will do nothing but increase his thirst.'

He realised from the start that he was making a mistake in marrying Cecilia but within a few years Benjamin had also been born and James had four healthy, bouncing Jewish children, which had been the whole purpose of the exercise. He didn't talk to anyone about his feelings and about how he pined all day and every day for the girl he had met when he was a kid, his first and only love, but he certainly wasn't a good husband. Like so many of the married men that he knew and did business with, he had affairs and spent as much time outside the home as he could find excuses for.

'None of the affairs meant anything,' he says now, 'Because none of the girls was you.'

He would go to strip joints and lap dancing clubs in desperate attempts to put off going home, to distract himself and forget how unhappy he was, although he would never screw the girls there. He is totally not into paying girls just for a fuck. He went on long business trips alone, some of them lasting three months or more. He became overweight and he was drinking too much, not in euphoria, as we did when we were together, but to try to escape from his own thoughts and to help him get through another miserable day. Unhappiness takes a terrible toll on your body.

* * * * * *

The day I gave birth to Hannah I felt that I was suffocating, while simultaneously being overwhelmed with emotions of joy. The physical part of actually giving birth was not a problem, but the moment I realised I now had the responsibility of a child it was like a terrible wake-up call. I became incredibly anxious that I might not be able to care for her.

When the doctor put her in my arms it was the most enormous feeling and I guess only other mothers can understand it. As soon as the baby lies on you your husband becomes number two in a fraction of a second. As soon as Frederic took her in his arms I wanted to snatch her back from him because she was 'mine'. I don't know why women become that way, but they do, they just become weird and the relationship between the mother and her husband changes in a huge way. The temptation to criticise everything they do with the baby, to contradict and nag, seems irresistible – although I was never going to turn into a monster wife like Cecilia.

What is it with marriage? I know so many couples who are going along together perfectly well and as soon as they get the rings on their fingers marriage sucks them into something they didn't realise they were signing up for. Suddenly they find they 'belong' to each other and what do you so often end up doing when you own something? You start treating it differently, less respectfully, less carefully.

Immediately after my wedding I had started wanting to have a child because I was so bored with my life and lonely and because I could hear the steady tick tock of my biological clock as I approached thirty. I craved something to distract me from the feeling of disappointment that shrouded all my waking hours. I had enjoyed the party after my wedding, but since then life had been completely flat. What did I have to look forward to? What did I have to distract myself when my husband was out working all night? At least a child, I told myself, would be company. And of course many of my friends were giving birth by then so it seemed like a natural thing to do. After an initial miscarriage I finally got pregnant two years after the wedding. I gave up work for a while, so that I could concentrate on Hannah.

But once I actually had the tiny, beautiful creature in my arms I realised that I had trapped myself. I now had a child to take responsibility for. I could no longer just expect to be able to please myself, not even in my fantasies. I was now set on a course of life which I had not really wanted, which actually precluded everything that I longed for. I felt all the natural urges to love and protect my child, even though I was never going to be someone who makes their children the sole purpose of their lives, but it was as if my eyes had suddenly been opened to the reality of how my life was going to be from then on. I could now see, with a blinding clarity, that I was no longer free, but what could I do about it?

CHAPTER SIX

Lugano is not a big place. Not that many people live there and although I didn't know it, James was asking after me, hearing everything I was doing, following what was happening in my life. He could never resist asking after me when he met any mutual friends, even though hearing about me increased the pain of not being with me, reminding him of just how unhappy he was in the life he had chosen. He was always thinking about me, asking about me, remembering all the times we had made love, reliving every sweet, sensual moment of being together, imagining what my life must be like now and what it would be like to be with me again, touching me again, looking at me, talking to me, just being in my presence. We were still so close even when our lives were so far apart.

He heard about Hannah's arrival but he did not make contact, respecting my wish and maybe protecting himself from the pain of acknowledging that I had given birth to another man's child. I can understand exactly how painful that was for him, having suffered the same thing every time I heard that Cecilia had given birth. Coming out of a pharmacy in the centre of town one day, however, we bumped into one another and he stopped to talk, although both of us were in a state of tongue-tied shock to find ourselves together after eight years of not speaking.

'This must be Hannah,' he said and I was hardly able to take in what he was saying, completely unable to think of anything to say in reply as a million different emotions swept over me.

I was shocked to see him and even more shocked to find he knew my child's name. Remembering how I felt when I first saw Isaac I could imagine how painful that first encounter was for him. Seeing her in the flesh was confirmation that another man had penetrated me, had been to the places that were most private and which he still wanted to believe belonged to him alone. Hannah was living proof that I truly had another life without him, inhabited other bedrooms and enacted other love scenes. I had a child with another man, an intimate link that he could never hope to break. I could recognise all those thoughts as they crossed his face and tightened his throat because I had experienced them all myself, many, many times. Such thoughts bring on a pain so unbearable it is hard to find the words to even speak. His heart was racing as fast as mine as we struggled to find the right things to say.

Later he told me how I struck him that day. 'You were still the most beautiful creature I had ever seen but now there was an air of sadness about your eyes and your posture, and in the dowdiness of your clothes. It was as if you had lost the sparkle that had lit your face when you were young. You looked as if your bloom had deserted you, like a beautiful houseplant in need of light and water. It wasn't just a physical thing, not just the way you were dressed and the sadness in your face, it was a mental thing, like you had shut down and given up on life and fun.'

The awkwardness between us was still as intense as it had been when we had been trapped together listening to

Cecilia breastfeeding on the nursery intercom. I fumbled with opening Hannah's pushchair and my hands were shaking, as were his as he tried to assist. We exchanged a few banalities and then hurried away from one another, neither of us able to cope with the pain for a second longer.

When Frederic eventually quit his night job and started managing a hotel restaurant instead I was ready to go back to work and went to work with him. We still needed two incomes. Now we could be together far more, and that was when the cracks in our relationship really started to show. As long as we were leading separate lives I had been able to fool myself, and most other people, that things were okay and would one day get better. We fell into a new rut of working every day, all day, still never having any fun together. He didn't like to travel so we never went anywhere on vacation and we worked in the hospitality business so we never went out to dinner. I was desperately unhappy to think that this was what my life was going to be like till the end, but I couldn't see any way to change it now that I had a daughter to look after and protect. And anyway, what were the alternatives?

The hotel, and especially the lobby bar, was well known in the area and it was inevitable that James would come there eventually. When I saw him walk in for the first time, not having seen him since the awkward encounter outside the pharmacy, my heart started to thump with exactly the same excitement I had experienced when I was fifteen years old. We spoke for no more than ten minutes but I knew that nothing had changed in my feelings towards him, and it probably never would.

* * * * * *

'You will never guess who I bumped into,' Kate said, 'your old friend, James.'

Kate was the one crazy girlfriend left in my boring married life and her insanity kept me at least a little sane. The chaos of her life distracted me from the terrible monotony of my own. She had just been to a wedding in Los Angeles and had phoned me the moment she got back.

Just the mention of his name and instantly my heart was pounding in the same way it always had when he was around. I listened to her telling me how great he was and about the crush she had developed on him, but only half my mind was with her. I could imagine what a bad state he was in mentally by now because of the pressures of his marriage, so I could also imagine how he might have allowed some spark to happen with Kate because however insane she was, she was attractive, with an incredibly infectious laugh. She was the sort of woman he was more likely to want to have a couple of margaritas with than sex.

'We're meeting for lunch today,' she said.

'Great,' I replied, as casually as I could manage, 'why don't you meet at my restaurant? It would be nice to see you both.'

They came for lunch and I served them myself, struggling all the time to make out it was the most normal thing in the world, keeping my face like a mask. It had been eight months since I had seen him last, but still he had the same effect on me. I didn't mind the fact that he was flirting with Kate because I knew that ultimately she was not his type, and anyway he was still married to Cecilia and I took some comfort in this proof that things were not going well there. Just to be able to see him and talk to him again was enough to lift my spirits. We were all chatting happily then Kate announced that she had to go. That was fine by me. Frederic was working in the kitchen and the lunchtime rush was nearly over so there we were, the two of us sitting at a table just as I had dreamed of a million times. We talked for two hours, exactly as we had when we were young. I couldn't believe I was really sitting opposite the love of my life and my best friend again. Only later did he tell me what had happened at the wedding in Los Angeles.

He had been socialising at the bar by the beach, even though he hates having to make small talk at formal events like that, when a striking girl came up to the man he was talking to. Although Kate wasn't his type, she is certainly nice to look at. The man introduced them and James saw a look of surprise pass through Kate's eyes when she heard his name.

'Do you know Penny?' she asked.

'My heart speeded up just to hear your name,' he told me, 'and I felt a bubble of joy rising inside me.'

'Yes,' he replied, trying to keep calm.

'She's my best friend,' Kate said.

'Now she had my full attention,' James said, leaning closer across the table. 'I had seen another possible way back to seeing you again. The next morning I saw her in the lobby of the hotel and the first thing I asked was, "did you tell Penny you bumped into me?" "Yes," she said, "I told her, she was amazed." I felt an enormous surge of joy, as if I had suddenly been allowed back into the best game of my life.'

None of this he told me as we sat in the hotel restaurant. Just as we always had, we both avoided saying the things that we most wanted to say to one another for fear of what forces we would unleash. Frederic finished in the kitchen and came out. I introduced them since they had never met properly. He didn't seem remotely interested in this man who was monopolising his wife's attention and went off to do the accounts, knowing nothing of the history that lay between James and me, leaving us still talking and staring into one another's eyes, catching up with everything that had happened in our lives since we last poured our hearts out to one another.

'Your husband doesn't know anything about your past?' James asked, amazed. 'Hasn't he ever asked you questions?'

'He's never been interested. He's not the jealous kind. I don't think he cares about my past, it has never bothered him.' As I said the words I could hear how sad they sounded.

James and Kate went out a few times after that, although they never got as far as sleeping together. They were both so screwed up at the time I could see it was never going anywhere, and their friendship allowed me to spend time with James without any pressure. Just having him in my life every now and then lifted my heart in the same way as a day in the sun or a bottle of Cristal. Never knowing when those moments would happen brought back the excitement I remembered from our early days of struggling to find time to be together during school days. But, just like in those days, I spent most of my time apart from him, feeling lonely and thinking about him.

'Do you mind if I screw James?' Kate asked one day.

'By all means,' I said, 'go ahead. I highly recommend him.'

I knew that it would never come to anything but when James heard what I'd said he didn't like it.

'It made me wonder if it meant you didn't care for me in

the same way I cared for you,' he told me later. He was confused by the contradictory signals he thought I was giving out, worried that perhaps he didn't understand me as completely as he had thought. I was so confused by that stage I didn't know what signals I was giving out to anyone. 'How could you have done that?' he asked. 'How could you have thrown me into another woman's arms?'

'Because I wasn't worried about you and her,' was all I said.

'I could never throw you into another man's arms,' he protested, 'I would die at the thought.'

I just shrugged, and left him to think it through for a while. Despite his being offended by that remark, he still came regularly with Kate to eat at the restaurant and I always ended up sitting at their table.

One day they were due to eat lunch together at a Japanese restaurant and they invited me to join them. Both James and I arrived early and Kate was delayed for some reason. We were talking intensely as always.

'You know,' James said after a bit, 'wouldn't it be cool if Kate didn't show up and we could just have lunch together?' We burst out laughing, knowing that we had both been thinking exactly the same thing.

He could see my answer in my eyes. Whenever we were alone together it was like we were back in the same exclusive bubble we had inhabited when we had first met and first made love. It felt like nothing else in the outside world mattered as long as we were together, staring at each other, talking to each other, longing to touch one another. Every so often I would force myself to look away, frightened of giving away too many of my feelings. I couldn't stop imagining what his body would look like, how it might have changed since I last saw and touched it, feeling horribly jealous of the women he had been with since we were last together. Did he want me as desperately as I wanted him? How would I survive the rest of my life if he didn't? Was being his friend the most I could ever hope for now?

Although I told him that I was not worried about him sleeping with Kate, I was very pleased when he refrained from doing so. I knew that he was not a faithful husband, but I also knew that he would never lead another girl on to believing there was some sort of future for them with him if there wasn't. He was always very open and honest about all his intentions, always willing to own up to his mistakes. It was another of the many things that I adored about him.

Despite the fact that we were back in touch, we were both still trapped in our unhappy situations. But simply re-establishing contact, and realising that nothing had changed between us, was like opening a window and letting a gust of fresh air into a room which had grown stale. Being able to sit next to one another and look into each other's eyes now and again was enough to re-invigorate us. This reminder of how great life could be increased my determination to do something about removing the weight of unhappiness that was constantly crushing my heart and my spirit. It was like the scales had been lifted from my eyes and I could see clearly that I had never met any person in my life with whom I was so totally comfortable and whose company left me so elated, and certainly not Frederic. From the first day I had met him in the coffee shop James had been my soulmate and nothing had changed.

His relationship with Kate began to cool but for more than six months James still came to the restaurant virtually every day as if drawn by a magnet, unable to stay away. If he had a business lunch he would arrange it there, and if he didn't have a business lunch he would come alone just to be able to look at me as I worked and talk to me if there was an opportunity. I could feel life and love and laughter seeping back into me, waking up parts of my brain that had dried up and shrivelled away to nothing. I noticed he was starting to take more trouble with his appearance, losing a little weight, shaving with more care, putting on ties. He later told me that during that period he would wake up in the morning feeling excited and would book his table at the restaurant as soon as he reached the office, even though he never usually books anything in advance, preferring to live spontaneously in the moment.

I also started taking more care of my appearance again. Every morning, when I first arrived at the restaurant, I would ask if James had reserved for lunch. My heart would lift when the answer was affirmative and sink a little if he had not yet rung. One day he had to cancel and I felt my newfound happiness lurch dangerously close to the edge, threatening to slip back into the black hole it had been in for so many years, a little voice at the back of my head warning me that I was vesting too much in this one relationship where I had no control and where it was unlikely that anything could ever develop. But I couldn't stop myself. I actually cared deeply about something again. I was coming alive, having fun. It was like a whole new game was starting and it felt fantastic.

CHAPTER SEVEN

Frederic and I were getting ready to go out for a friend's birthday party when our marriage exploded into the biggest argument we had ever had. Ignited by something trivial it opened the floodgates on every grudge we had both been harbouring. Apart from our personal differences the business had also been struggling and we'd had to take some hard decisions like moving to a smaller apartment. He found it hard to cope with having to step back financially. He found adapting impossible. All the unhappiness and resentment that had been building up over the previous few years erupted to the surface and it was clear that we had reached the end of the line, saying things to one another that could never be taken back or forgotten. Forty-eight hours later, after he had shouted at me in an aggressive and scary way, I left with Hannah.

Frederic had recently come into some money and we had bought a small apartment that we intended to do up and move to. He hadn't set foot in it since we bought it, so I took Hannah there to give myself time to work out what I was going to do next, aware that I might not be able to stay there long if he wanted to sell up. The only thing I knew for certain was that I couldn't continue living the life that I had and I didn't want to be with him for a moment longer. But at the same time, how would I survive as a single mother?

Two weeks later, when emotions between us were already running at fever pitch, he confessed that he had been having an affair for six months with one of the employees at the hotel. For me this was more proof that he had no respect for me and we had merely been enduring our life together out of habit. To my surprise the discovery of the affair did not make me feel any worse, if anything it confirmed that I was making the right decision by following my instincts and walking away. However intimidating the road ahead might look, there was no possible way back now and that felt like a relief.

Once I had found out the truth I took off my wedding ring. It seemed such a stupid symbol now. What had it been for if not to show to the world that he was 'my husband', but even that hadn't been true because he had been sleeping with someone else. He had broken my trust and behaved like an asshole, the diamond had been a complete waste of money, as arbitrary and meaningless as a red rose on Valentine's Day. My memories of my wedding day, the big party and the beautiful white dress all meant to show the world that we belonged to each other seemed like hypocrisy now.

Even though I knew it was right, leaving was an enormous decision because Hannah was now two and a half years old and she wanted to be with both her Mummy and her Daddy. It is impossible to break up a family without causing drama and unhappiness, however much you might want to. At the same time it was a relief to be able to have Hannah to myself, not to have to answer to anyone else about what I chose to do with her. We were used to spending time alone together anyway because Frederic was always out at work, (or in bed with someone else), and I now had the freedom to go out with her wherever and whenever I wanted without asking for approval or giving any explanations.

As well as moving out of my home I was also walking out of my job, because I worked with Frederic, without having any other source of support in place. It would have been a great deal easier just to have kept on putting up with being unhappy, which I knew was the decision many of my friends who were in bad marriages were making, but I wasn't willing to do that any longer. I was literally throwing myself over a precipice into the unknown, with a child to take care of and no idea how I was going to do that. I had a friend in Washington DC and I wondered if perhaps I should go out there and start my life with Hannah again from scratch.

A few weeks later James got to hear that I had left my marriage and made contact as a concerned and sympathetic friend. He phoned me on my mobile while I was driving.

'So,' he said, 'It looks like you might end up being divorced before me.'

'It seems so,' I laughed.

He invited me out for lunch at a well-known Italian restaurant in town.

'I want to talk to you about Kate,' he said.

'What's up?' I asked. 'Did she get lunatic on you?'

I didn't care what he wanted to talk about, I was just excited at the thought of being able to see him and talk to him again. He was, after all, the man who knew and understood me better than any other person on earth. I had no particular plan for trying to rekindle our relationship because I was in shock from the abrupt ending of my marriage, and because I didn't know if he would ever leave Cecilia and the children – but I still went to the hairdressers before the lunch, just to be sure that I looked my best.

I knew that Kate was becoming hysterical in the relationship because James hadn't phoned her for several days. She'd asked me to talk to him about it and I told myself that was a good pretext for accepting his lunch invitation. There was so much to talk about, but still so much that we weren't yet ready to deal with in our own lives. I was now in rather an awkward situation with Kate, who was longing for information about her own relationship with James, which I knew perfectly well was never going to go anywhere.

James had taken a discreet table in the far corner of the restaurant, one of the many places in town where he was well known.

'Listen,' he said once we had sat down and ordered, 'I need to explain to you why I haven't phoned Kate.' He had the same boyish grin that he'd had when he was seventeen. 'It's because I've found someone new that I really like.'

I felt an icy shiver running through my entire body. Kate was no threat, I knew that, but now there was someone else? He was watching my eyes and saw the reaction, which seemed to amuse him. It was like he was playing a particularly high stakes game of poker but I couldn't be sure what cards either of us was holding. I must have allowed my disquiet to show in my eyes.

'I'm joking,' he said, as if to pacify me, 'but not joking. There is someone I am interested in.'

What the hell? What was I doing sitting there in front of him? I couldn't work out what he was saying exactly. There were too many different thoughts and emotions already coursing through my brain to be able to work it out, I just knew that when he looked at me with his piercing stare I wanted to melt into his arms. When he grinned I just wanted to kiss him. I had so much to think about. I was still trying to work out the best way to deal with my separation and with Hannah. On top of that I was coping with pressure from my father, who wanted to take over sorting my life out for me, and from my parents-in-law, who wanted me to go back to Frederic. I didn't have any spare capacity for playing games like this. I didn't ask any more questions and we talked easily about a thousand different things, a welcome distraction from the turmoil going on inside my head.

When we finally had to leave the restaurant he walked with me to the car park where I'd left my car, but I couldn't remember which floor I'd left it on. He came into the elevator with me and the tension between us was so thick you could have cut it with a knife. I longed for him to kiss me and I knew he wanted to, but neither of us was sure how the other would react if we made the first move. The doors of the lift opened and we both stepped out quickly, avoiding one another's eyes. As I walked ahead I felt his eyes following me, conscious of the sound my heels were making on the concrete floor. I couldn't see the car; it must be the wrong floor. We were going to have to get back in the elevator together. I was becoming flustered and forced myself to remain calm. We got back into the elevator and went to the next floor, the tension had increased a hundredfold.

Only later did James confess that he had been trying to pluck up the courage to kiss me, frightened of rejection but promising himself that if we got back into the elevator one more time he would do it. I found my car on the next floor and drove away, leaving him feeling angry with himself for losing his nerve.

* * * * * *

We met for a second lunch in another restaurant the next day and in between we had started messaging each other regularly as friends. I told him I was planning to take Hannah off for a holiday at my friend's house in Washington DC, in order to take some time to get my thoughts together and work out what I wanted to do. I had sold some jewellery and a dress to buy the tickets and to give myself some spending money for when I got there, but when I told him that we were going to be flying economy James was horrified.

'Long haul with a child?' he said, genuinely aghast. 'It'll be hell. Believe me, I travel a great deal with children. You'll be jammed in the middle seats between two enormous men. I have plenty of air miles; let me upgrade your tickets.'

I was touched by his obviously genuine concern. He also offered to lend me money.

'It'll just be repayment for all the pizzas you bought me when we were in school,' he joked, but I didn't feel it was right to take his money.

He truly was the best friend I had ever had. My father had given me his credit card numbers so I could have upgraded at his expense, but I didn't want to do that either. He was under the impression that without a husband I would automatically revert to being a child who needed his protection. It was a view that Frederic shared. Both of them seemed to have forgotten that I had been supporting myself ever since I left college and had every intention of continuing to do so. I wanted to take responsibility for my decisions, and for looking after Hannah and myself. An upgrade using a friend's air miles, however, seemed like a kind gesture and I thought it would be churlish to say no. Once we'd finished eating James took me to the smoking room where there was a computer, but he wasn't able to do what he wanted because he didn't have his pin number. I could see how disappointed he was, and how tempted he was just to buy us tickets, but he too could see that that would have been inappropriate for the delicate new balance that our friendship was now finding.

'I promise I will have sorted it out so that you are at least upgraded on the way back,' he said. It was so cute that he was so concerned and wanted to take care of Hannah and me.

This time as we parted and he went to kiss me on the cheek, he allowed his lips to linger and I felt a huge charge of electricity pass between us.

As I walked back to my car, which was parked about a hundred yards away, James stood rooted to the spot, watching me, imprinting every movement of my body on his memory. I told myself that if I looked back when I got to the car and he was still watching me then I would know that something was going to happen between us. At the last moment I turned, our eyes locked and I felt my heart soaring as I climbed into the car and started the engine.

A few moments later my phone buzzed with an SMS.

'What just happened, Penny?'

'I don't know,' I replied, 'I felt it too.'

The messages went on and on like we were two teenagers experiencing our first major crushes. He told me that he too had decided that if I turned round and looked back it would mean that I was still interested in him, and I knew instantly that when he had talked about having someone new he was interested in he had been talking about me. From that moment we were messaging each other constantly, as if an emotional dam had burst and every pent-up emotion, dream and thought was now able to flood through.

* * * * * *

The following day we were lunching together again and I could feel the excitement building inside me. Something enormous was happening. I could feel it as surely as the tremors that come before an earthquake. Now I wanted to be with him every second I could, but I was going to be flying to the other side of the world for a fortnight in two days' time. Should I cancel the holiday? He also had to fly to London for a meeting and I could see that he didn't want us to be apart now any more than I did. Now we were able to talk freely about our feelings and we couldn't even be bothered to eat the food that was being put in front of us, talking, talking all the time.

'Listen,' he said, eventually forcing himself to look at his watch, 'I have to buy a computer for Isaac before I go to London. You go home now and I'll get a taxi back to your apartment and leave it there.'

I drove the twenty minutes home hardly able to breathe. He was actually going to be coming to my house. This seemed like another gigantic step into the unknown, but at the same time a step back into the comforts and pleasures of the past and the fulfilment of a thousand dreams and fantasies I'd had over the years. Once I got home I was pacing from window to window, just as I had done the first night he came to me in my sister's apartment. Hannah had gone to the park with the nanny, (the only thing that I had allowed my father to pay for and to be honest I don't know how I would have managed without her), so I had nothing to distract me from the waiting. Already he had the habit of being constantly in touch through messaging. He kept sending messages from the taxi, 'ten minutes away', 'five minutes away'. Then he realised he only had pounds in preparation for his trip and the driver was going to need Swiss francs. I went to the door with my purse and he was there, standing on the doorstep, having managed to persuade the driver to take sterling.

As soon as I shut the door behind us he dropped the package onto the floor and pushed me against the wall, kissing me for the first time since we were at school, unable to hold himself back for another second. I couldn't breathe but I didn't care. It was as if all the weight of the previous years had lifted from my shoulders and freed my heart to soar. As I felt the familiar softness of his lips on mine and tasted his tongue it was like returning to the surface after swimming underwater for fifteen years. He was the oxygen I needed in order to survive. Everything was exactly as I remembered. His skin still smelled the same as I had remembered. It's a magic skin, always smelling good. It was a kiss like you see in the movies but seldom experience in life. If it had been a movie there would have been fireworks filling the sky. In my stomach it felt as if I had just dropped off a cliff and was falling back into the past; falling, falling. Nothing had changed – nothing. Everything was going to be all right.

Unable to tear ourselves apart we moved as one person into the elevator and I scrabbled to press the button. I heard the doors close and felt us rising to my floor. We were still entwined as we fell through the apartment door, neither of us able to believe that so many years of suffering could finally have ended in this explosion of desire.

He stayed for about half an hour as we kissed and held each other, neither of us ever wanting to let go, both of us knowing that however ecstatic we were at that moment we still had a long way to go before everything would be smooth for us. Frederic had never set foot in the apartment since the day we bought it, so I felt like I was becoming an independent woman again, but James was still living with his wife and four children. I knew how unhappy he was with Cecilia and I was now beginning to feel more confident of how he felt about me, but I still didn't know if he would ever be able to bring himself to leave the kids and defy his family. All this could still come to nothing and I would be plunged back into the black hole I had been living in for so long.

'I no longer care what my father thinks about what I do,' he told me during one of our endless conversations. 'I know he had no ill intentions when he sowed those seeds of destruction in my mind, but I am no longer willing to be miserable. He has four wonderful Jewish grandchildren, and I would not have wanted my children to be any different to the way they are either. But there is nothing else for me to stay in the marriage for now, apart from keeping up appearances. I no longer care what anyone thinks, except for you.'

I understood exactly what he meant because we both knew so many unhappily married couples who were doing exactly that, keeping up appearances, hanging on to the familiar. He had been through an unbearable fourteen years but now, hopefully, the ordeal was about to be over. Perhaps that was the moment when he became a grown up and finally took his life into his own hands.

CHAPTER EIGHT

From that first kiss inside my front door my heart felt it was being torn in two. I wanted nothing more than to be with James but I couldn't cancel my tickets and I didn't want to disappoint my friend. She had told me repeatedly how much she was looking forward to seeing me. We hadn't seen each other for years because of my work and my marriage. I hadn't even managed to get to her wedding, even though she was my dearest and closest friend. So although I didn't want to be parted from James for even a minute longer than I had to be, there was no way I could cancel. I also knew that with so many things going on at once it would be good to take the opportunity to have some time away to think things through.

The day before we were both due to fly out of the country we wanted to be close. James booked a hotel room, ordered Club sandwiches and we lay together on the bed, just holding one another, talking and kissing. We undressed so that we could feel one another's skins and be as close as it was possible to be, but we kept our underwear on, as if saving something for later, not wanting to rush and spoil things by going too fast. We didn't want our renaissance to be only about sex, we wanted it to be about closeness and intimacy first, knowing that would make the sex more special when it happened. The room was a hundred times more beautiful than the rooms we had hired when we were at school, but the excitement of being there together felt just the same.

Coming back from the hotel room lunch with James I was just so happy to have found him again.

I hardly had a chance to watch the road as I drove home because of all the messages that were flying back and forth between us, but it would have been impossible to resist them, however dangerous the drive might become. We missed each other so badly already, and we knew the time change was going to make communicating even more difficult.

Once I got home I packed our suitcase and prepared everything for the next day. The flight to Zurich was early and from there we had a connection to Washington DC.

James's first messages of the day started to arrive even before my alarm clock went off. He was so concerned and so caring that our trip should go well that I could tell he ached to be with me as much as I ached for him.

'You know, I have taken a plane with my daughter before,' I said when he called me for the twentieth time while I was checking in.

'I know, I know,' he laughed. 'Sorry. I just want you to be okay.'

He was so used to making all the arrangements and taking care of Cecilia, who was incapable of being a grown up, that he was finding it hard to imagine that I was capable of doing anything. It would take him a while to learn that not every woman was like her.

The wait in Zurich seemed endless and at least a hundred times I decided to cancel the whole trip, inventing a story as to why we wouldn't be able to take that plane. Unaware of all the thoughts racing through her mother's head Hannah was becoming more and more excited about the long plane ride that lay ahead of us.

Hannah's passport was included in my German one, but just in case I had put her Swiss passport in my bag as well.

'I'm sorry, Madam,' the official told us as we got to passport control, 'Your daughter's passport is not valid.'

'Why not?'

'This is a child's passport in yours, which is not valid for the USA.'

'Grab this opportunity, Penny,' a voice in my head told me. 'Don't mention the Swiss passport, just turn round and go back to Lugano.'

My hand took no notice of the voice, pulling Hannah's valid document out of my bag and passing it over. 'Does this work?'

'Yes, Madam, this is perfect. Have a good trip.'

I couldn't do it. I had to do what I had promised to do. I had to do this trip and wait a few more days to be with him.

I missed him so much and the fact that he was messaging me every five minutes, asking where I was, if I was at the gate and how everything was going, just made it worse. I could picture him sitting on his own, staring at his phone thinking about us as we went through all the familiar airport routines. I didn't want to shut down my phone. The thought of twelve hours without contact was unbearable. We finally got to the gate.

'I have to switch off my phone now,' I messaged.

'I love you,' he replied, using those words for the first time. My heart leapt but I then had to shut off the phone, knowing that I wouldn't be able to talk to him again until we landed.

My head was buzzing with confusion as we struggled

onto the plane. Our seats were in the middle of a row, with big men on each side, just as James had predicted, but Hannah behaved like an angel and I had twelve hours of almost uninterrupted thinking as I tried to work out what I was going to do with the rest of my life. I had ruled out any thoughts of going back to Frederic, but I was going to have to find some way of earning a living and I had to decide what I would do if James did not in the end leave Cecilia. I had earphones on, listening to music. Madonna was singing, 'time goes by, so slowly...' and I knew exactly what she was talking about.

When we finally arrived in Washington my friend was waiting for us at the airport, waving excitedly. I guess she had expected to be meeting an emotional wreck.

'You look great, Babe!' she said as she hugged me. 'I thought you'd look like a zombie.'

'I feel great,' I said, with a huge smile. 'I will get a divorce.'

'Oh my God! Awesome,' she said and we both burst out laughing at the same moment.

* * * * * *

I was very happy to see my friend. She was in great shape, married to a wonderful guy and they had a two-year-old son. Even though my head was full of James, we had a great time and the kids had lots of fun. Jet lag made things difficult. Hannah would get up in the middle of the night and walk around during the wrong hours.

James and I were constantly in touch throughout the days. Now that we were reconnected we wanted to be talking every second of every day. Texts flew back and forth and, when the time difference allowed, we spent long hours on the phone, talking about the past and the future, how we felt and how much we missed each other. The crazy kiss at the apartment and the afternoon together in the hotel had been so wonderful that being separated again so soon was agonising. Both of us just wanted to drop everything and be alone together. I cut my stay short by two days, telling myself I didn't want to be a burden on my friend, but actually just desperate to see him again. He had gone from London to Israel and was now sending texts counting down the hours till we could be together again.

'When you come back,' he said, 'why don't we meet up in Zurich and book into a hotel, just for one night? Could you organise the nanny for Hannah? I don't want to separate you from her if it is too complicated.'

He was right, it was difficult to leave Hannah with our nanny. She was jet-lagged, and still so small and I felt guilty leaving her at home and not telling anyone where I was going. At that time I wasn't on good terms at all with Frederic and I would never have asked him to have her. He wasn't really in a fit state at that time to take care of her, having gone completely weird. It would be nearly a year before he started taking his fathering responsibilities seriously and taking Hannah two weekends a month. Even then I wasn't always comfortable leaving her with him. He was still with the woman who he had betrayed me with and I didn't like the idea of her looking after my daughter at all.

Three days after returning from Washington, however, I was waiting for James at Zurich airport. I had packed my little bag – my God, why is it so difficult to pack a little bag for one night? What should I wear to bed? What to wear to go out at night? In the end I packed a pair of jeans with a fancy, floaty top and some high-heeled boots for the evening, a tiny pair of shorts and T-shirt I had bought at Victoria's Secret the week before in the sales and a set of fresh, cute underwear. I just wanted to be me, how James knew me.

My stomach was aching with nerves, alternately staring at the Arrivals doors and frantically messaging as he drew closer, watching the endless lines of people coming through, thinking that the agony of waiting would never end. I didn't see him coming because I'd forgotten he'd told me he'd had his hair cut. Suddenly I felt someone lifting me into the air and kissing me with such passion, swinging me round with such joy.

'You like?' he asked, touching his hair with a shy smile after putting me back down.

'I like,' I assured him, 'I like very much.'

What was not to like? He was the most gorgeous guy to me. His hair had been growing long before but now he had told his barber to cut it short, as if to shed the past and start afresh. He looked younger, healthier and happier than I had seen him for years. It was like a symbolic turning of the page. Although I didn't care what length his hair was as long as I could be with him, I liked the idea that he now looked different to how he had looked all the years he was with Cecilia.

'How was your flight?' I asked.

'Much too long! I couldn't sleep because I was so impatient to see you.'

He took my hand and placed my bag on his rolling suitcase as we rushed out of the airport. In the taxi we couldn't stop smiling and kissing. We were so happy but there was also a cute shyness between us, knowing that we were going to be spending our first night together.

'Is Hannah okay?' he asked. 'I hope you feel okay to have left her. I don't want you to get into trouble or anything.'

'Does your wife know where you are?'

'Yes, in Tel Aviv. I didn't tell her I left already.'

'But she'll call the hotel and find out you're gone...'

'I don't care. I have my phone off. I'll handle it tomorrow, now it's "us" time. I've booked us into a very nice hotel, you'll see.'

At the reception I hovered a little behind to give him some privacy while discussing things with the concierge and check-in people. I could hear he was asking for an upgrade and I heard that he had asked the price for a suite. I could vaguely hear the price that the receptionist mentioned and it was outrageous. I knew James wanted it all to be special and at that moment he would have bought the moon for me if it had been for sale – that felt very good. It felt good to have someone who cared about me, who cared about my wellbeing and who wanted to please me.

There was an awkward moment of silence in the elevator as the receptionist took us up to our suite.

The bedroom was huge and fantastic with two bathrooms and a living room. It was all very modern but in an ancient building so it had the mixture of new and old that I love. Once the receptionist had left us James took me in his arms and kissed me for the longest time. We just stood there and clung to each other.

'Where do you want to eat dinner?' he asked eventually.

'I don't know Zurich well and frankly anything is fine with me.'

'Why don't we just go down to the bar for a drink and eat here in the hotel restaurant?'

'Fine with me, good idea.'

I couldn't have cared less where we went, we just wanted to be together and not lose time sitting in taxis and fussing with reservations. I prepared myself, took a shower, put on my jeans and my top. I applied some discreet make-up and brushed my hair. When I came out of the bathroom James was standing there with a huge smile.

'You look fantastic,' he said. 'So pretty.'

'I just have to quickly call Hannah and see if everything is all right...'

She was okay. I could hear her voice in the background as I quizzed the nanny as to whether she had eaten and whether she was ready for bed. She put Hannah on the phone and I spoke to her and she seemed happy. That was all I needed, just to feel relaxed about her and not have any stresses.

Downstairs in the bar the 'happy hour' was already in full swing and businessmen were standing around in suits and loosened ties, sipping their cocktails. We sat down and ordered a good white wine. I didn't know that James was into white wine. When we were together at school we had hardly enough money for beer and now he was contemplating the wine menu, asking me if I liked a Chablis better or a Pouilly Fumé.

'Since when are you into wine?'

'Being married to Cecilia, I need to drink a lot,' he laughed.

'I love Pouilly Fumé.'

The entire evening we couldn't stop talking. We had so many questions for each other. I was speaking a lot about my work since I left university, the job I had loved so much and the hard times afterwards in the hotel with Frederic, how it all fell to pieces because of his low management skills and his big ego. He spoke about his kids, about Cecilia and all the horror and fighting he had been through. We poured out our hearts, needing to rid ourselves of all the heavy stuff we had been carrying on our shoulders. Hours later we went upstairs to our room and when I came out of the bathroom in my shorts and T-shirt, he smiled, took me in his arms and kissed me.

'I don't want anything to happen tonight,' he whispered in my ear, 'I just want to hold you and feel your skin.'

I let myself dissolve in his arms and inhaled the scent of his skin.

'I missed you so much,' he murmured. 'Every year you become more beautiful, more sparkling and more desirable. Every day I am newly stunned by how fabulous you are.'

'I missed you too.'

'I missed you all my life. I should never have let you go.'

'I know, but I'm here now.'

We slipped under the covers and turned off the lights. The room was totally dark and we could hear ourselves breathing, just enjoying this moment of being finally together. No sneaking out, no hiding in classrooms, just two adults in a hotel bed for an entire night. I couldn't stop grinning. James stood up and went to the bathroom, coming back with my Body Shop body cream.

'I want to massage you,' he said, 'just to feel your body and your skin.'

I pulled off my T-shirt and he started stroking my back with the cream. As his fingers glided down my spine I turned around and we kissed. We kissed with such passion in that dark room, both our hearts beating fast. We hadn't been like this since before he met Cecilia and we were longing for each other. James had said that we didn't have to make love that night and that we could wait, but I needed and wanted him so badly. I had longed for him every second when I was in Washington. I just needed him inside me and to feel him as close as I could. He slid off my cotton shorts and kissed me all over. Our bodies were on fire. It was so dark that we could only touch and feel but not really see each other's faces, but I knew we were both entirely happy. I felt his erection sliding into me and we lay still for a while, just wanting to feel our bodies conjoined. It was like coming home. It was like when we made love the first time but now I had a woman's body. I had been thinking of this moment my whole life and here it was. I had him back inside me and slowly, gently, we started to move together.

It didn't take us long to collapse into each other's arms, both breathing heavily. We squeezed close and talked for a while, unable to believe what had actually just happened. I was slowly falling asleep in his arms, still feeling him caressing my hair and breathing in my ear as I drifted off.

* * * * * *

'Good morning,' he said when I next opened my eyes and found his smiling face watching me. 'What would you like for breakfast?' He looked like a little boy. He had the cutest smile and I had never seen him look so happy.

'Just black coffee and some pastries,' I said.

As we waited for room service we both took showers in different bathrooms and came out into the salon of the suite in fluffy hotel bathrobes – the sort you always want to steal from five-star hotels. Breakfast was all laid out and waiting.

I was lying on the couch with my head on his knees as we giggled, eating croissants and soaking up every minute we could before we had to take the train back to our real lives. He teased me about the way I spread the jam, never having had breakfast with me before. It was an intimate moment we had never been able to share in the past. It felt like everything had fallen into place but at the same time we knew it couldn't last, not yet.

'Penny, it's time. We need to catch a cab to the station. If you want to be home by four we need to go. If I switch on my phone I'll probably have three hundred missed calls from Cecilia.'

We spent the entire train journey cuddled together, neither of us wanting to let go. We occupied our seat as if we were one person, our limbs entwined as I dozed contentedly with my head against his chest.

'Can you believe it's us?' James asked; a question that we kept on asking each other as our story progressed.

It was Saturday and we knew we wouldn't see each other before Monday. It seemed like forever. What would I do with Hannah the next day? Weekends were so boring and my head was so full I didn't know if I could cope with being the mom bouncing a small child around in the park on my own for hours.

James had to leave the train first and then I would get out at the next stop. We kissed and kissed and he stepped out, standing on the platform looking at me through the window. The train started rolling again and I saw him saying something. I could read his lips and see the sentence they were forming. He was saying, 'I love you' and then he disappeared from sight.

CHAPTER NINE

Now that I had taken the decision to divorce I wanted to arrange things quickly and I immediately hired a lawyer, which seemed to surprise Frederic. Until that moment I'm not sure that he really believed I was serious about ending our relationship for ever, as if I had been bluffing in some way. He did try to make me change my mind, but it was too late, I was already far, far away from the marriage in my head.

Throughout that summer James and I spent as much time together as possible, which mainly meant lunches. Sometimes he would have commitments at home or business which meant that we would be unable to see each other for anything up to forty-eight hours, a horrible ordeal every time, although slightly alleviated by our new habit of constant messaging back and forth. James had to prepare the ground for leaving Cecilia and although I trusted him when he said it would not take more than a few months, I knew that many married men believed the same thing and in the end never managed to make the break from their homes and children. Whenever we met he never tried to hide me away in unknown places, he was very fair and open about everything.

'Cecilia and I are already sleeping in separate rooms,' he assured me, 'and we have been for some time. I promise you we will never be sleeping together again, but

I just need time to sort out the business side of the divorce before I leave.'

Inside my head I decided that if we weren't together within a year I would walk away. I certainly did not intend to spend the rest of my life being 'the other woman' however much I might love him, although I couldn't imagine how I would cope with the pain of parting from him again. Most of the time I felt confident he would not disappoint me, but I knew so many men who were having affairs and who never actually left their wives. How could I be sure if he would ever make the big step? But at the same time I knew he didn't want to stay with her for a moment longer than he had to.

Normally each summer he would take his whole family away on holiday, but that year he didn't go. Even then I couldn't shake off the constant state of anguish I felt that he and Cecilia might just go off for a weekend together and my fragile new bubble of joy would be popped forever.

'I could not do that to you,' he said. 'I could not have you spending weeks imagining me away on holiday without you, not even for a day.'

One night during those months of waiting my doorbell rang unexpectedly and I found him on the doorstep in sweat pants and flip-flops.

'What are you doing?' I asked, feeling both shocked and thrilled to see him unexpectedly, so happy I was bouncing about like a puppy.

'I told Cecilia I needed to pop out for cigarettes.'

'But it's a half-hour drive to get here! You have to go back right away. Your phone will ring in a minute.'

'I just wanted to kiss you,' he said, with such a happy smile.

'Okay,' I laughed and ushered him in. We sat on the sofa and he kissed me and I was flooded with all the same excitement I felt every time his lips touched mine, like we were still teenagers exploring one another's mouths for the first time. I had just put Hannah to bed half an hour earlier and prayed she wouldn't wake up, not now...

'Can I just lie down on your bed?' he asked after a while.

'Why?' I asked.

'Just in case. I need to know what it feels like.'

We lay down together, peacefully entwined in the same way we had always been whenever we had a chance.

'Turn off the light,' he said.

'But you have to go back.'

'I need to know what it really feels like.'

The next thing we knew it was eight o'clock in the morning. As he hurried from the flat he turned on the doorstep and grinned like a happy schoolboy.

'How good was that?' he asked and ran to the car before I could answer.

We both knew exactly how good it had been. I had taken one step away from the abyss of misery that had been threatening to swallow the rest of my life. I still did not yet know what the future held for me but at least now I was free to dream. Luckily Hannah was still asleep by the time he left. If she had seen him in the bedroom at that stage it would have been a disaster. There were so many ways in which our bubble might be burst at any moment by the realities of our daily lives.

All the things about James that turned me on when he was seventeen still turned me on when we came back together, and still turn me on today. He is now twenty-four years older than when I saw him in the crowded coffee shop and his body is a little more fragile, but to my mind that makes him even more manlike. His brain and his humour have grown sharper with every passing year, which makes him much sexier than the eager young boy who first swept me off my feet. Humour and smartness are a million times more exciting than perfectly toned muscles and perfectly combed hair.

He still dresses the same way as he did when we were kids and I love that, always wearing good jeans with a turtleneck or shirt and blazer. One of his trademark pieces is a sleeveless down jacket, which he wears all the time. He simply has no fashion issues because he is so comfortable with who he is. He could live without a mirror and would still always look immaculately handsome.

* * * * * *

All through the many months of lunches we talked about our future together. Things were becoming worse and worse for him at home and the tension with Cecilia was at the highest and shrillest point ever.

'We hardly exchange a civil word,' he said. 'We fight like animals all day long. I think she knows that I'm planning to leave.'

'Does she know about me?'

'No, I'm sure she doesn't.'

That summer was the best and worst of my life. We enjoyed every minute we were together but whenever we were apart it was horrific. The loneliness was physically painful and it was difficult for me to take care of Hannah as well as I wanted to because I was always juggling the nanny's hours with the ones I was able to see James.

I constantly had to improvise at the last minute because he found he could stay longer with me and we wanted to enjoy every minute. I was lost between wanting to give my life a second chance with James and the relationship we had dreamed of all our lives, and wanting to be a good mother to Hannah. I was very unhappy in the moments James wasn't with me, and scared as well. What if he didn't leave Cecilia? Nothing is ever certain and I had just escaped a failed marriage so I knew how hard it was to make the final break. He was going to be leaving behind four children so that was never going to be easy for him if it did happen. What if it didn't happen? What was I going to do with my life, with my daughter? I felt helpless and was often too anxious to sleep.

The anxiety wasn't helped by the fact that I was also fighting with Frederic as we disentangled ourselves from the marriage and having to attend stressful meetings with lawyers that frequently left me weeping in my car afterwards. The only times either of us were free of stress was during the hours that we snatched together on James's boat or over our long lunches.

Modern technology meant that at least we could be messaging one another, and we both had our phones in sight every minute that we were apart, but whenever he didn't respond right away I knew it was because Cecilia was around, which was like a knife in my heart each time I pictured it.

The weekends were the worst. He couldn't lunch with me on weekends and even though he did not take his family on holiday, he still gave the kids a good time on the lake and obviously I knew their mother was there as well. Forty-eight hours without seeing him, knowing they had to do activities together with their children and afterwards see mutual friends. It was like torture.

* * * * * *

One of the first things James did once we were reunited was take me to Israel, and there we did have to hide away, big time! He wanted to show me the exact place where he was when his courage failed and he did not ask me out for a holiday after finishing his exams, as he had promised.

We had to travel in secret since James was still officially married and living with his wife and children, which made it seem all the more exciting and heightened the emotions. I hadn't told anyone where I was going. Hannah was staying with our nanny and I felt a little guilty about leaving her. I had also lied to my father, telling him I was going to Italy, since Tel Aviv was not the safest place in the world during that summer. I was barely talking to Frederic at the time and so I hadn't even told him I was going away. All these things were weighing on my conscience but I was still determined to go. I wanted to give myself a second chance. I reasoned that it would benefit all of us if I could repair my personal life and that spending four days with the nanny she knew and loved was not going to do a three year-old girl too much damage. Despite all this logic, I still felt a pain in my heart as I said goodbye to my sweet, trusting little girl and was fearful at the thought of being a four-hour flight away from her.

Despite the furtiveness it felt to me like a symbolic victory to finally be able to go there together as a couple. He showed me the place where he would have been sitting when we spoke on the phone, when he was so torn between his duty to his father and to his Jewish heritage and his own emotions which screamed out for him to be with me at every moment until death finally claimed one or other of us.

'It now seems impossible to believe that I ever managed to ignore those voices,' he said, 'that I had ever for a moment thought that I would be able to thrive without you. I want to take you to the Holocaust Museum in Jerusalem, so you will understand. It is the first thing anyone should do when they visit this country because it will give you a different perspective on everything.'

The following day a chauffeur drove us up the hills towards the city of gold with the city of Ramala on the left. The heat was suffocating, about thirty-five degrees, and I changed into long pants in the car because after the museum we were going to the Wailing Wall. I was jumping about like a kid on holiday; I was in Israel with James!

As we approached the buildings, which harmonise so perfectly with the ancient architecture and landscapes of the city, I could already feel the emotions rising up to choke me. Even though James had talked about his own visits there, still I was not prepared for the shock of actually walking into the building and seeing the evidence of the atrocities laid out so lovingly and reverentially.

There was so much to see, each exhibit more overwhelming and heart-rending than the last. It was impossible to take it all in and impossible to hold back the tears. In one showcase was a huge, beautiful necklace of diamonds and emeralds, the sort of thing you might buy at Cartier and would only wear to a grand ball. Below there was a sign telling the story of a man who had given this necklace to his wife for her birthday. When the Germans came to get them he hid it under the parquet floor in the dining room. His wife was brutally murdered in a concentration camp gas oven and when he finally returned home at the end of the war, having lost everything, the necklace was still there. Not having the heart to sell it, the family had donated it to the museum.

As we walked on through the rooms I stopped speaking, there was nothing to say in the face of such overwhelming sadness. I held back the tears until we reached the children's memorial, but I could not control them any longer as we walked through a black corridor into the large circular room with one candle at the centre. Cleverly placed mirrors reflected that candle into one and a half million lights, paying tribute to the one and half million children who died. I sobbed silently as a voice intoned the name, origin and age of each child. Even when we were finally back in the car it was still impossible to speak. I have been back several times since and each time the effect is just as devastating.

James would say that marrying someone other than me was the worse decision of his life, but we will never know what would have happened if things had gone differently. Would our relationship have survived our immaturity and the pressures of early marriage and children? Would we have what we have today if we had not been through the hell of those fifteen or so years of self-inflicted separation? We lost so much during those years, but we did gain wisdom. We learned what was most important and we learned how to ensure we kept alive what was most precious to us.

Although I have no strong religious feelings myself, I couldn't help but be moved by the Wailing Wall. It is a huge experience and a very private place despite the crowds that always throng there. I have now been at least nine times and each time I am newly awed by the atmosphere and the feeling that comes over me when I touch the stones and feel their history float into me, giving me goosebumps and always bringing tears to my eyes. It feels as if someone or something bigger than us resides there. Visitors are supposed to write wishes or messages on little bits of paper and wedge them between the stones. You can see thousands of them peeking out from all over the wall, and the belief is that when your message falls out your wish comes true and your message is heard. I love that idea and James and I always write our messages and wishes in the car when we get there, not showing them to one another like excited children. Whenever I walk away from the Wall, backwards as is the custom, I always have a smile on my face, no matter what emotions I have been through in the previous hours.

* * * * * *

'We are landing in ten minutes, ladies and gentlemen,' the stewardess on the flight back from Tel Aviv announced, 'please fasten your seatbelts and put your chairs in the upright position.'

'I've made a decision,' James said, taking hold of my hand and looking directly into my eyes. 'I'm not going back home. Can I move into your apartment tonight?'

'Of course,' I could hardly breathe at the thought of such a dramatic change to everything and I leant towards him, kissing him gently on the lips, unable to think clearly enough to speak.

He squeezed my hand comfortingly as the plane started its descent. I looked out of the window. Seeing Lugano approaching I wondered what was going to happen once we arrived. It was awkward. It felt weird to imagine James would just come home with me, leaving our wonderful days in Israel behind and returning to the reality of our everyday lives.

He slept at my place that night, but we didn't make love, the air was too heavy and there was something that didn't feel right. It was like we were living in limbo, on the cusp of a new life but still not safely there yet. There was so much that could still go wrong, so much pain still to go through. The same awkwardness was there the next morning as he left for work and we agreed to meet for lunch. There was a weird atmosphere between us that neither of us could put into words, as if something was about to happen.

* * * * * *

When I arrived at the restaurant I felt unaccountably nervous: something was up and I felt James was not himself.

'What's wrong with you?' I asked. 'You seem preoccupied.'

'You know, Penny,' he said. 'I want to be with you every day of my life. I will never let you go again, ever. But...' There was a terrible pause when I felt the bottom falling out of my world, 'I need to do this the right way. I can't walk out just like that, I need closure. I need Cecilia to know exactly why I am leaving and how it's going to happen.'

He saw the tears rising in my eyes and took my hand, pressing it against his face. I felt a wave of terror rippling through me. Was he getting cold feet? Had he changed his mind now that we were back in the real world, away from the romantic cocoon we had inhabited in Israel, with all its heightened emotions?

'It is going to happen, Penny,' he said, 'I promise. I just need a few more days, please.'

I couldn't say anything, I just nodded and the rest of our lunch was quiet. I knew he was being sincere but my heart felt weak. I was so sad and started to really doubt that my sadness was ever going to end. We spoke a few times during the day and when I came out of Hannah's room after she had fallen asleep that night, I heard an SMS arrive on my phone.

'I am going to sit down now with Cecilia and talk to her. I won't be able to SMS any more tonight. Sleep well Love.'

Oh my God! What was going to be said between them? I wanted to be a fly on the wall. How would I ever be able to sleep tonight?

The next SMS didn't come until seven the following morning.

'Good morning.'

'How was the talk?'

'Good, tough, long but not finished yet. Let's meet for lunch at 12.30.'

When I arrived at lunch I was aching with nerves. I couldn't wait to hear every word that was discussed. I needed to know exactly what was going on.

'I sat her down and I started from day one when we met,' he said. 'I told her I didn't want her to speak. I just wanted to explain to her, detail by detail, what she had done to me. I wanted her to understand how unhappy I was, how we fought, how evil and disgusting she has been, how she puts me down all the time, how she never supported me in my career, never attended dinners with clients. How she threw tantrums when she didn't get a present, how I had to sell my car because she wanted to go on vacation one summer.'

He poured out everything, wanting her to understand why he was leaving, not wanting anybody to think he was deserting his family because of a fling with a blonde girl. He needed this closure in order to be free. It was Friday and he wasn't done yet. He hadn't yet finished what he had started.

We kissed goodbye at the end of lunch and hugged for a very long time before I left for town to do some shopping and headed home to see Hannah.

* * * * * *

It was the longest weekend I can ever remember. The next day he took his family out on the lake, played with his kids, made them a barbecue and once they were all in bed he sat down with Cecilia again and continued where he had stopped the night before. He talked through the entire night again.

The next morning the family was ready to leave the house to go back to the lake but James didn't make any signs of going with them. He took Cecilia into the bedroom so the kids couldn't hear anything and explained that he was leaving that day. He told her that he had met me again but that I wasn't at all the reason why he was taking this decision; he just wanted to be the one to tell her that he was with me. Shocked, Cecilia took the kids and rushed out.

My phone rang at ten o'clock in the morning.

'Hi,' I said and my voice was trembling.

'Hi,' he said. 'I guess I did it.'

'Where is everybody?'

'She took the kids to a friend's house.'

'Should I come over and pick you up?'

'Sure.'

A heavy silence fell. I couldn't find the words. There was nothing I could say. I felt terrified for him, for me, for his kids, for all of us. He was out. What happened now? What to do on a Sunday? Just us. It felt like we had been beamed into an alien situation and we needed to work out how to handle it. We were starting from scratch, like newborns.

Was my home his now? Would he feel at home or would he miss the house he was used to? We both felt so happy and yet so disoriented. We spent the day out with Hannah, tiptoeing around, trying to find out what we were feeling. I felt so guilty that he was having to be with Hannah, having just had to part from his own kids, not knowing what his relationship with them would be like in the future. But we had to face the reality; we were two very responsible parents and adults so what had just happened to James that Sunday morning was a huge step into a new life, filled with complications. We could see that there was a lot of suffering ahead, but now I could see that there might be a lot of happiness at the same time.

That night when we went home he said he wanted to make us some dinner. He was standing in my kitchen trying to figure out where all the utensils were, trying to look at ease. He caught my eye and we both smiled at the same time because we knew that he had never opened a drawer in this place and that he was lost.

'Where do you keep your onions and garlic?'

'Onions and garlic? I don't have onions and garlic.'

'So, how do you cook a tomato sauce?'

'Without,' I laughed.

'Oh, Penny,' he laughed too, 'I really have to go and get you some real food.'

He managed to make us wonderful pasta with the little I had and we had a quiet dinner, talking over everything that had happened and basking in the pleasure of being together. All the time his phone was vibrating with vitriolic messages from Cecilia. We knew the next months and weeks were going to be hard, especially for him. This was just the start of a huge divorce battle with children involved, a crazy ex-wife to handle and a job to do in order to earn enough money to finance the whole process. At that moment I didn't care about any of that because it felt like all my dreams had come true and all the pieces in my life had come together. With him beside me I could face anything.

He had only brought a small suitcase with him, enough to dress himself for the coming week. He didn't care about the stuff he had left behind.

'I want to buy everything new,' he said, 'and get rid of everything from the past that I'm leaving behind.'

Even though I wished sometimes that he had brought all his belongings with him and had made the final break, I came to realise that this was a much nicer way to arrive in a new life, empty-handed so that we could build up our lives together, day by day, piece by piece. It made us less scared about all the huge changes that would be happening, and it meant that things just fitted in smoothly, like the pieces of a puzzle.

My Germanic sense of order meant I would have loved our life together to be all set and running from the first day, with his books and DVDs installed on my shelves as a sign that he was really there to stay. But it wasn't like that. I learned patience. I learned that personal belongings are not in the least bit important, that if you are in love you don't care about those things. I learned that sharing bills and organisational chores, as one does in a marriage, is actually more of a hassle than anything. We didn't have any of this together. I had my things to take care of while he took care of his and it was good this way. It is still the same way today and James and I never fight about bills, money or anything to do with the household. We don't put ourselves under any unnecessary pressure because there is enough of that around us already.

CHAPTER TEN

Despite being so completely in love, I was still nervous, as well as excited, about how living together full-time would work out. Frederic had agreed to allow me to have full custody of Hannah, although he now wanted to have her to stay with him as often as possible, which I was happy to encourage. I had just escaped from living with someone and had started to enjoy the feeling of independence and not having to consult anyone else about every tiny decision I made. Was I ready to give up that freedom so quickly, even for James? He and I had never lived together as a couple; would too much familiarity ruin everything we had? Or would it be the greatest thing that could possibly happen to us? How would he fit in with Hannah? How would she react to a virtual stranger coming into her home? What would she think when she woke up in the morning and found him in my bed, a man she had spent no more than an hour with in total up until that fateful Sunday morning when everything changed forever? How did he like to live on a day-to-day basis? We knew so little about one another's daily lives. I didn't even know what brand of toothpaste he liked.

All these questions and uncertainties descended on me at once, mixing with the euphoria of actually having him there with me and knowing that he wouldn't be having to dash away in a few hours' time, and threatened to suffocate me in a mixture of joy, excitement and trepidation.

The fact that he had arrived on my doorstep with only one suitcase was so romantic. After so much sadness I felt like a weight had lifted from my shoulders and I was the happiest person on earth. At the same time I was aware that as long as so many of his possessions remained in the marital home he had not moved out completely. I loved it when he said he was not interested in any of the possessions that he and Cecilia had accrued during those miserable years together, and I soon discovered that he meant it when he said he had no interest in things like clothes, being perfectly happy to buy new ones if he needed them, but still I was aware that as long as he was living out of a suitcase he could disappear from the apartment as quickly as he had arrived.

Slowly however, day by joyful day, week by exciting week, month by wonderful month, he settled in. One day he would start to use a drawer for his underwear, another he would use a section of the wardrobe for his suits. All the time, however, he was careful to stress that it was my home and that he didn't want to rush me into anything too fast. I wouldn't have cared how fast he had rushed me and I adored him all the more for being so considerate of my feelings.

True to his word, when Cecilia did start to send over suitcases of his things he threw them away, saying, 'I want nothing from the past.' I realised that he truly couldn't have cared less. He didn't even open them to see what was inside, just gave everything away. I liked that. It made me feel good that he was starting afresh and I followed his example, getting rid of some of my old things too.

We were both in the dark about how our divorces would eventually turn out, having no idea what the final settlements would be or how high the lawyers' bills would rise before everything was resolved. The uncertainty was hard for James. There were some nights when he would wake up drenched in the sweat of anxiety attacks as he imagined how it might all end for us and for his children. I wasn't so worried, as long as I had him with me. I knew from past experience that I could always make a living when I needed to and would be able to support Hannah whatever happened.

My divorce was going ahead much quicker than his and I understood completely what he was feeling and, although I would have preferred to live without the uncertainty, it really didn't bother me. I knew he was going to have to work hard to generate enough money to live over the following few years, supporting his kids, his ex-wife and our household, but I didn't expect him to be my protector. It turns him on to think he is and I like it that he wants to be, but he's not. He makes me feel cared for and secure and that is very sexy, but I will always want to maintain my independence, an attitude which he also finds sexy, and totally unlike most of the women he has known in the past. In fact I was lucky and I didn't get back to work for two years after leaving Frederic, wanting to take time for Hannah and time to build my relationship with James. It's hard to do all three and my priorities were Hannah and James.

James's assurances that I was not the reason for his leaving the marriage did not convince Cecilia. She assumed that I was the reason for the break up and waged open war on me for at least a year, screaming abuse down the phone all day long, even scraping her car along the side of James's when she saw me sitting in it. She kept the kids away from him as much as she could, which made him sad, but he didn't fight too hard to start with, giving her time to calm down and for the situation to settle. It was a period of enormous turmoil for all of us. My divorce took two years to finalise, but his took five and even at the end of it Cecilia still rang constantly or had her lawyers send fresh demands. It was hard, but we felt able to face any amount of stress and be happy as long as we had each other, as long as we could hold one another in bed, talk to one another all day long, kiss and touch and make love.

* * * * * *

There was so much we needed to learn about one another as we started to share our lives. I found it very weird that James had turned totally kosher in the years that he had been with Cecilia. It was the biggest thing that had changed about him. The boy I had known had been a total ham eater. So many afternoons after school we would joyfully share pizza prosciutto and I just couldn't understand how that could have changed so completely.

I was talking to him on the phone as I walked round the supermarket, grabbing the usual salami for me and Hannah, and the hot dog sausages she loved so much, just thinking of filling up my fridge as usual.

'What kind of non-pork stuff do you eat?' I asked as I continued to shop.

'Just get me some Bündnerfleisch and that fantastic Findus Lasagne, please... that was not allowed in my house.'

'Lasagne is beef,' I said.

'I know, but it has cream with it, so it's considered not kosher.'

'Oh my God, she really did fuck up your brain.'

I respected his beliefs totally and didn't comment on them again, but I could see so many times the looks that he gave my salami in the fridge when he decided to make himself a sandwich, as if he was having to battle with invisible demons in order to keep his hands off it. I knew deep down that he was feeling an inner conflict. There was the part of him that didn't believe in the concept of kosher food, but at the same time his kids were being brought up this way so he felt guilty towards them, as if he was betraying them in some way when he did non-kosher things. I knew it was hard for him and I knew I had to let him handle it his own way while continuing to buy food that was fun for all three of us at home.

After we had been together about a year we were in a very cute pizzeria outside Lugano after a day trip. I ordered a big salad and was shocked to hear James say to the waiter, 'a margherita for me with extra prosciutto, please.'

I looked at him with raised eyebrows.

'Don't talk,' he said.

'I wasn't going to,' I replied and tried to catch up on a conversation we had started before in the car about the children and their different characters.

A few minutes later the waiter placed that pizza in front of him. He took the first bite and looked as if he had just been released from prison. Expressions of relief and joy spread across his face as he tucked in.

'Are you okay?' I asked once we were walking back to the car.

'I have never felt better in my life,' he replied and suddenly hugged me very tight. 'I am so happy to have you back. What the hell did I do all those years?'

'So you will eat pork again now?'

'Oh yes, Penny. Believe me, I will!'
'Welcome back!' I laughed. 'I love you!'

* * * * * *

In many respects James and I were still the same people who fell in love when we were fifteen and seventeen years old and our new situation offered us an opportunity to make our relationship into anything either of us wanted it to be without any of the pressures that would have been put on us had we still been teenagers.

James's career as a lawyer had been going well through the years of his marriage, partly because he was so happy to travel on business at the slightest excuse in order to get away from home, but once I was back in his life it was like his brain had woken up, his energy levels surged to extraordinary heights and he found he was suddenly being a hundred times more successful than he had ever been before. Now he had a reason to go to work every day; he wanted to impress me with everything he did and he wanted to succeed. He wanted to 'wow' me. Cecilia had never shown any interest in his work, all her energy went into the children and the family and herself, but I was fascinated by everything he did, everything he said, everyone he met. I had worked ever since leaving college and understood the world of business well by then. I was hungry to learn more. I wanted him to be able to discuss anything with me and I would be able to form opinions. We could talk and debate for hours and neither of us would ever take offence at anything the other might say.

We agreed from the beginning that neither of us would ever interfere with the way the other was parenting their children. Hannah was tiny when she was born, weighing less than two and a half kilos. She looked so fragile it was a little frightening in the beginning and stressful as I tried to bring her up to a good weight. When I left Frederic she obviously had trouble coping and didn't eat very much. When he came to live with us James could see I was struggling with my little girl and without me ever asking he started to help me out. I never asked for help, but he would just take over when he saw I was having problems and I totally let him because I knew he was a great dad.

Seeing that she wasn't really eating much he started cooking for her at night, enjoying introducing her to different tastes and making food a joy. Without ever making a big thing of it he has been instrumental in teaching her the pleasures of good eating. He has taught her what food is about. Today Hannah is a gourmet. If it's bad food she doesn't eat it, but if it's good then it's a pleasure to watch her cleaning her plate. I love that about James. For him it's always been very important that his children discover foods and cultures from all over the world and when we travel he takes huge pleasure in going to restaurants that serve Chinese, Japanese or Thai food. Even if we're going for hamburgers he takes time to find the best burger places in town and turns dinners into festivals for all of us.

When he decides to prepare a special dinner he watches a dozen different cooks doing the dish in different ways before setting about it in his own style. He watches cooking like a maniac and uses Hannah and me as his guinea pigs. He'll go to the best butchers and grocers, buying far too many ingredients. He buys kitchen knives like he's a three-star Michelin chef. Everything he does he does with such passion and such gusto. Just watching him makes me laugh and fills me with pleasure.

One night when Hannah was delirious with a forty-degree fever, talking nonsense with her little body burning up at four in the morning, I became scared, not knowing what to do for the best. James just put her in a bath of the perfect temperature and sat with her, gently bathing her until she cooled down. He did it with such gentleness and such ease it took my breath away.

I would never ask him to pick her up from school or to bring her somewhere. I would never ask him to help her with homework or any of the hundreds of other daily parenting duties, so when he steps in so naturally I know it's because he really wants to and he always surprises me with his parenting skills. I respect the fact that he does not live with his kids any more and can't take care of them on a daily basis and so I would never ask him to take care of mine. I understand it must be painful for him sometimes and I would never expect him to be Hannah's dad.

CHAPTER ELEVEN

It was a long time before Cecilia accepted that I could see James's kids. There were many painful fights with James over whether 'the blonde bitch who took her husband away' was good enough to spend time on holiday with 'her' kids. It didn't look like James was ever going to be able to persuade her that he had been going to leave her anyway, that I had nothing to do with it. Eventually, however, she consented to him taking them on holiday and to me being introduced.

'We should do this in a cool and smooth way,' James said over dinner one night as we went through possible hotels and destinations.

'I don't think I should come for the whole ten days the first time,' I said. 'I don't think Cecilia would accept that anyway. Why don't I go to Spain to see my parents with Hannah for a couple of days? Then I'll drop her at Frederic's and meet you wherever you are.'

'Not a bad idea,' James said as he thought it through. 'So I'll find a place that suits everyone, doesn't cost me a fortune, and which you can easily get to. Somewhere that can do three rooms in the middle of the high season.'

'What on earth made you decide to make so many children?' I laughed.

He rolled his eyes and heaved a deep sigh, a sound that I knew so well, one that I heard so often, whenever Cecilia's vitriolic messages and letters arrived, and one which he didn't have to explain any further. It means, 'Why the fuck didn't I tell you that I loved you when we were first together, and why did I ever marry that woman? I should never have let you go.'

'Italy!' he said after a few minutes of research. 'Check out Italy!'

'That's cool,' I said, 'I can easily come there.'

'Or the kids and I could do five days in Italy and then you could join us later for a few days. At least then you and I can go out at night.'

So it was settled and a couple of months later James and the kids headed off to Italy for the longest five days I had had to endure since going to America without him. We hadn't been apart for a single day since he had moved in with me and the thought of being apart for even five days dragged both our spirits way down. James was excited to finally be able to spend some time with his kids the way he wanted, without having Cecilia getting lunatic and ruining the trip as she usually did, but he too dreaded us being separated.

We were both nervous about how the kids would deal with meeting me, knowing that they would never have heard their mother saying a good word about me. They were bound to be expecting the worst. It seemed very unfair that they had to cope with an adult's ego trips and jealousies and I was sure they would be watching my every move with understandable suspicion; I was after all 'that blonde who had stolen their father and broken up their home'.

After a pleasant few days with Hannah in Spain, I left her with her father and flew to Olbia, feeling increasingly sick with nerves. I took a cab from the airport, taking in the beautiful scenery as we sped along. We had chosen a hotel that although a little touristy in high season has an amazing pool that would keep the kids occupied during the day. I wanted to be able to take time off on my own if things turned bad or the atmosphere wasn't good. It seemed important not to go anywhere we would all feel trapped together twenty-four hours a day and the area offered a great many compensations for adults, pretty much like living on a real-life James Bond set.

Arriving at the hotel I booked myself in and James sent a message to say they were all down by the pool already. This meant that the first time the kids saw me I was going to be in a bathing suit – an intimidating prospect for someone who is already feeling a little vulnerable. I changed in the room and made my way down, trying not to look nervous. I could see from the twinkle in James's eye as he scanned my body that at least he was pleased with the effect. As soon as we had finished saying 'hi', Rachel and Claudia immediately went off to make phone calls and I guessed they were reporting back to their mother on what my figure looked like and taking a guess at my weight.

It must have been obvious that I felt awkward in the situation, although I tried really hard to act cool, and was careful to make sure I took a back seat to them when it came to monopolising James's time during the day. Whether they liked what they had seen so far, I must still have seemed like a threat, like the wicked woman who had made their dad leave them.

Both James and I were longing to hug and kiss, having missed one another painfully during the previous five days, but we obviously couldn't do that to the children. That would have been way too much, way too soon. We were aching to talk, but we couldn't really do that either because the children were around all the time, listening and wanting to talk themselves, climbing all over their dad, craving his attention, calling out his name every few minutes. I was suddenly in the middle of a whole new world. Used to being with my quiet little daughter I had to adjust to so many people at once – wow! All I wanted was for them all to disappear so that James and I could be together in privacy, but I knew that wasn't the deal.

That evening we all went to a nice Italian restaurant and to my surprise I found I was actually having fun with them. The ice was beginning to melt and we were all starting to relax.

'Let's go to a club,' James said when we got back to the hotel and the kids disappeared off to their rooms. 'We can grab a drink and talk. I need to feel older than twelve for a few hours, right now. I've been missing you all day.'

'Can you leave them without a babysitter?' I asked.

'Sure, they're big enough. There's four of them and if there's a problem, believe me,' he waved his phone in the air, 'I will be made aware of it in a second.'

'Well then, let's go!' I said, excited that we were finally going to be alone together and eager to taste a bit of the local high life.

Ten minutes later I had redone my make-up, pulled my shoes back on and we were in a nearby club ordering a bottle of wine. It was much too crowded, being the mid-August peak season, and you couldn't even reach the dancefloor, but we didn't care. We talked and drank for two hours before deciding to go back to the hotel. I went straight to the room while James popped into the kids' rooms to check they were okay.

'All sound asleep,' he reported as he came into the room,

closing the door behind him and taking me in his arms. He kissed me softly on my neck and my lips, then began to undress me slowly.

He produced some new velcro bondage straps and held them up with a cheeky grin on his face. Immediately intrigued, I did as he asked without questioning what he was planning and stood naked in front of him for a moment, enjoying him staring at me, knowing he had something in mind.

He lay me on the bed and spread my legs, brushing his hands across my skin as he strapped my ankles and wrists to the bed ends with the straps and tied a blindfold around my eyes. He said nothing else, still giving me no idea what he might be planning. He was still fully dressed. This was getting really interesting.

My limbs were pulled out so tightly on the bed I could feel every muscle on the inside of my thighs stretching. I sensed that James had stood back to stare as the veins pumped away beneath my skin, my arms pulled out to the sides, my breasts thrusting upwards. I felt incredibly vulnerable and I knew how much he would be wanting to screw me. Why was he holding back? What was he doing? What was happening?

I heard the clicking of a camera shutter, the sound of a chair being pulled up close to the bed, then silence.

'What are you doing?' I asked, my head jerking from side to side as I tried to work out where he was in the room.

'Shh,' he said, very quietly. 'Don't say a word.'

I thought he must be sitting on the chair beside the bed, staring at me in the light of one bedside lamp and a muted, flickering television screen. The tension was building as I twitched and struggled against the bonds. My breathing was becoming faster. I heard him pick up the phone and dial.

'What are you doing?' I asked again but he didn't answer.

I pulled against the straps, testing their strength, every muscle tense with excitement. There was no way I could escape.

'I would like a bottle of Chablis,' he said. He was talking to room service.

'You're not doing this,' I said, aware of my heart beating so fast in my chest that it must be visible through the taut skin above my breast, but I didn't tell him to stop.

'Now that you've said that,' he said, 'I'm doing it.'

He must have had his finger on the button. He'd been faking. Now I heard him dialling for real. This time I could hear the answering voice as he ordered the wine. It made me struggle again against the straps, but still I didn't tell him to stop. If I told him to stop I would never know how the scene would play out. Once he'd put the phone down he fell silent again and I knew he was watching me, saying nothing. I could feel that I was growing moist between my legs and knew that I definitely wouldn't be telling him to stop now, however anxious I might be growing.

'What are you doing?' I wanted to know. 'I can hear your breathing so I know you're there.'

He said nothing. Realising that he was not going to respond, I too fell silent as we waited together. It was now around four in the morning, room service was not going to be working at full stretch so we shouldn't have long to wait.

After a few minutes I heard a tap on the door and still I didn't know what he was going to do. Perhaps he would just open the door a crack, take the tray from the waiter, sign and pass him some money, or maybe he would invite him in. I could hear him walking across the room. I heard his hand on the lock and felt a slight draught as he opened the door wide and ushered someone in.

'Put it there, please,' James said, and I heard the rattle of ice cubes shaking in the bucket as the waiter saw the vision pinned out on the bed, my heartbeat as visible as my glistening pussy. I was straining to work out what James was doing, instinctively struggling again to free myself. I heard the sound of another man swallowing loudly as he put down the tray and tried to find his voice.

'Can you please sign here?'

'Open the bottle, please,' James said, his voice deliberately calm and as exquisitely polite as ever, like an actor inhabiting a role.

I was twisting my head frantically from side to side, searching for clues as I tried to understand what was happening in the room from hearing alone. But now the only sound was the squeaking of the corkscrew turning in the waiter's sweating palm. I have never felt as purely naked and vulnerable in my life. It felt like the top layer of my skin had been stripped away, leaving me exposed to the core. The squeaking stopped and the cork popped out. There was the slosh of liquid going into a glass. He must be passing it to James to taste. I froze, not wanting to miss a single clue as to what might be about to happen.

'Oui,' James said after a few seconds, 'ça va.'

Was he going to ask the man to touch me and take the whole thing to the next level? How would the man react? What did he look like? I strained to work out what the sounds might mean. The man seemed to be pouring two glasses and presenting the bill for signature. I wondered if their hands were shaking. Was James smiling? Were they making eye contact? Were they exchanging signals? I thought I heard the rustle of money. Was he tipping him for the wine, or paying him for another service?

The man thanked him. I heard footsteps and the click of the door opening and closing. Then I heard the sound of clothes being removed and felt someone climbing onto the bed between my open legs. Someone took my chin between their fingertips and held my face still. James slid his tongue between my lips at the same time as guiding his erection into my pussy. It took only a few thrusts before we both reached our shuddering climaxes.

I'm always telling James that you should never regret anything, but once we had finished and were talking about what had happened he told me he regretted not having the nerve to push the possibilities of that scene a little further. Perhaps next time...

I wanted to know everything about the waiter, but all James would tell me, once he had untied me and we were drinking the wine, was that the guy was 'young' and 'not bad-looking'. The next day he refused to point him out to me or give me a more detailed description, so for the rest of our stay, with the children all around us, I was looking at every young guy working in the hotel. A waiter would bend over to serve me lunch on the beach or to refill my glass in the bar and I would be wondering if he was the one who had seen me naked and helpless, who had been so close to being invited to screw me. Would that scene now remain a part of his fantasies for the rest of his life?

Searching all the time for signs like a trembling hand, a half smile or a sidelong glance added an extra frisson of excitement to the following few days as we danced in the evenings and spent the days with the kids, eating in a local restaurant that had a terrace that opened to the blue

Mediterranean skies, gazing at the fabulous yachts, each one bigger and sleeker than the one before. Thoughts of that unseen waiter kept our horniness levels high for months after that trip was over.

CHAPTER TWELVE

'Go away!' I laughed as he hammered on the bathroom door.

'I want to see you!' he pleaded.

'You'll see me when I'm ready.'

I wanted everything to be perfect before I revealed myself to him. There would be no mystery if he saw how I was preparing myself and putting the whole outfit together.

My heart was thumping in my chest as the time of our departure from the hotel came closer. I was wearing a set of underwear that James had bought me as a surprise a couple of weeks before. He often surprises me with immaculately wrapped boxes from places like La Perla and Agent Provocateur, watching me open them with his naughty little grin. I slid on a pair of suspenders, something I don't usually wear. It was hard to clip on the stockings with no one to help with the ones at the back, and my hands were shaking with nerves, but I was determined not to involve him in the process. I chose a dark green, half-length Cavalli dress in a leopard print, which flowed beautifully against my legs and had a deep cleavage. The luxurious body cream I had used contained a dusting of gold powder, which made my arms and breasts shine in the discreet lighting of the bathroom. I pulled on very high, tight, black suede boots from Sergio Rossi and surveyed the results one last time in the mirror before unlocking the door. James was sitting on the edge of the bed, waiting patiently, and I knew from the look of wonder on his face, and the spread of his boyish smile that I had achieved the effect I wanted.

'Wow!' he said. 'Shall we go then?'

'I'm ready if you are,' I said, wondering if his stomach was aching with nerves in the same way mine was.

The whole adventure had started over dinner a few weeks before in a cute little neighbourhood restaurant in Lugano. It was a Friday night and we were both unwinding from a tough week.

'Have you ever heard of a prestigious swingers' club in Paris?' James asked. He mentioned a name I'd never heard of.

'No,' I said, looking at him quizzically. Just the thought of Paris was exciting in itself.

'It sounds very interesting,' he went on and his mischievous grin made me think he knew far more than he was saying. 'Very chic. Exclusive.'

We talked for more than two hours, ordering another bottle of Puligny-Montrachet as we tried to imagine what such a place might be like. What would the other people be like? What sort of things would they do? What sort of things would we want to do if we went there? Would it be dangerous? It was exciting just to talk about it and then we made a decision – we would go to Paris for a week and we would find that club. We wanted to have a holiday anyway after all the stress of the divorces, and James's business had been doing well. It was time to spoil ourselves a little after all we had been through.

I arranged for Hannah to stay with Frederic and we caught the train to Paris. I messed up with buying the tickets in some way and the carriages were so overcrowded we couldn't even find seats. Half the trip we were standing and the other half we were draped across the luggage racks, but we didn't care because we were together and we were going on an adventure. We were full of expectation for the delights and experiences the club would hold, apart from all the other pleasures that would come from a week in one of the most romantic and glamorous cities in the world. James hadn't been to Paris for seventeen years so it would be an adventure for both of us, regardless of what might happen at the club.

At the back of our minds, however, we were both curious about what went on behind the curtains in this mysterious club that was only ever talked about in whispers. Speeding through the French countryside, the thoughts of what might be lying in wait for us were making both our hearts beat with anticipation as we plunged towards the unknown. I felt the nerves tightening in the pit of my stomach every time I thought about it. Was this going to prove to be a mistake? Were we pushing the limits too far? What would we find waiting for us when we arrived? I was so excited.

James had booked us into the Hotel Meurice, one of the most elegant, glamorous and romantic hotels in the world. The luxury in our room was like a fantasy come true and we were both as excited as teenagers. It was because I was so nervous about what I was going to wear for the club that I had locked myself in the bathroom to get ready, refusing to let James in, no matter how hard he banged on the door or how abjectly he begged.

'The club is well known to every taxi driver and chauffeur in Paris,' James said as we descended towards the glamour of the lobby. 'As soon as we give them the address they'll know what we're doing.'

I shrugged. 'Then get them to drop us round the corner and we'll walk to the club.'

'No,' he shook his head. 'I'm not going to have you walking the streets at night. It would be too dangerous. If it's embarrassing we just have to face it.'

It was obvious from the raised eyebrow when we gave the address of where we wanted to go that the driver of the hotel limousine knew exactly what it was we were planning, but none of us said anything, him being too discreet and both of us being too tense for small talk as the car purred the short distance across night-time Paris to the narrow backstreet close to the Opera building.

The driver pulled up in front of a colossal, forbidding and ornate but unmarked pair of black doors that looked as if they had been built to repel an army. The air was cold as we got out of the car, our stomachs tight with nerves. There was no door handle or bell.

'Wait until you can see we are safely inside,' James instructed the driver.

As we got closer we could see that a smaller black door was cut into the big door and we let ourselves in. Inside was another locked door to be got through before we would finally be in the club. A camera was pointing down at us. As we came through the first door another couple stepped in behind us, nice-looking people, just ordinary like us. We were so tense at that stage we didn't even signify that the other couple were there, all of us averting our eyes, none of us knowing what we were supposed to do or what was lying in wait for us on the other side of the next door. There was a gold bell to ring and a sign reserving the management's right to turn us away without giving a reason, which increased the tension.

'Do you think they're watching us?' I whispered, huddling close to James for warmth and glancing up at the camera.

'Don't move your lips,' he muttered, 'just in case.'

I was close to getting the giggles, so I buried my chin in the collar of my coat and stared straight ahead. I could feel James bracing himself to put on the confident, charming front he always shows to strangers, especially when he is nervous.

After a few moments the second door opened and a stony-faced doorman appeared. He was slim and immaculately groomed, nothing like the usual mountainous club bouncers, but even more intimidating as he surveyed us all with a glacial, contemptuous stare.

'You two,' he said, nodding at the other couple, 'not possible tonight.'

The other couple slunk back out into the street, without even trying to negotiate or discover why they were being sent away, looking flustered and eager to escape from their humiliation.

'You two,' he nodded towards us, 'have you reserved?'

'Yes,' James said, having been warned by several people that it would be hard to get admission to this place even with a reservation, impossible without.

The man stood back and nodded us through, his face still unmoving, no glimmer of a smile. 'Names?'

James gave his full name.

'No surnames,' he snapped, 'just your first names.'

'Penny and James.'

The ancient brick walls were draped in red fabric and a chandelier sparkled above us. There were crystal bowls and plates of sweets laid out on tables, a buffet of haribos, pralines, jelly beans, marshmallows and fresh fruit platters. Perfumed candles flickered in every nook, delicately scenting the air. It was like a pornographer's interpretation of *Alice in Wonderland*, a castle tricked out to resemble a fantasy brothel. The doorman wrote our names on a card that had some sort of barcode on it.

'Give this to the barman downstairs,' he said and then walked off without glancing back, not even telling us which of the staircases we should go down.

I looped my arm through James's and we found our way down into a room with a bar and tables where we could obviously eat. Everyone in the room looked stunning; the girls looking like models, all beautifully dressed, the guys like James Bond. It was exciting just to be there, like taking part in a movie. The black velvet ceiling was buttoned with Swarovski crystals that hung down like snowflakes. There were bottles of Chanel No 5 and the most sumptuous hand creams in the ladies' powder room.

The food was perfect and as we ate and made nervous small talk we looked around, trying to become accustomed to our surroundings, trying to look like we belonged there. Music drifted up from the floor below.

Below us was the bar, beneath which a long mirror reflected the legs of women posing on stools in short skirts and no underwear, allowing us to watch a couple as the man's hand slid subtly in and out, exploring and playing along the woman's thighs and on up into the darkness beyond. We worked out there must have been two hundred people in the club that night, but it didn't feel full because half of them at any one time were behind curtains in the back rooms.

Once we'd eaten and talked and watched and fortified our spirits with a bottle of Cristal, we were ready to venture down another staircase, deeper into the throbbing, strobing bowels of Paris. On the dancefloor we were reserved and a little shy, glancing around to see what other people were doing before starting to let go. We danced for a while, our inhibitions loosened by the wine, until we'd pumped up some courage.

'You want to check out behind?' James asked, nodding towards the curtains.

I took hold of his hand and gave him a nod, letting him know that I was ready to step through the curtains into the unknown.

Inside the first room was draped in luxurious fabrics and sprayed with mint fragrance to sweeten the inevitable perfume that several dozen sexually aroused people were bound to emit. It took us a moment to adjust our senses to the new environment; the low lighting and the movement of strangers all around. We strolled about holding hands, forgetting to breathe and trying to look nonchalant as if we were on familiar territory, comfortable and at home, when in reality our hearts were thundering in our chests and we were looking around with eyes as wide as kids arriving in Disneyland for the first time. Slowly we were able to make out the people, some naked, some almost fully clothed.

We watched as half a dozen couples moved in and out of the melange of bodies on the bed, some screwing, some tasting, some stroking, some just watching or lying back and allowing other hands to caress them, other lips to kiss them and other people to screw them. Hands were sliding up and down penises, fingers tickling vaginas, tongues licking and tasting whatever took their fancy. There was no fear of upsetting anyone by staring, no pressure to join in with anything you didn't want to.

We stayed a while then strolled from room to room. Then we sat in the smoking room listening to other people talking, making a little conversation with other couples, drinking in the atmosphere, before going back into other rooms where different people had joined in the mix.

We wandered in and out of the rooms several times before we plucked up the courage to sit down on the edge of one of the sofas where someone else was making love and look more closely. It was the first time I had ever seen someone else screwing in front of me. This was not like watching actors in a porn movie; these were normal people like us, people with jobs and children and everyday worries just like ours, permitting us entry into their most private moments. The excitement and joyous freedom of it took my breath away. I felt strangely safe because there were so many women around and because everyone was equal. No one was judging anyone. No one was preying on anyone.

In another room there was an older woman with a beautiful young black man. They were surrounded by a small group of onlookers. We watched too because they were doing it so well, so stylishly, so sexily. As we stood together I felt a hand sliding over my breast and I squeezed James's hand gently to let him know something was happening. He glanced sideways and saw a beautiful Italian woman standing on the other side of me with her hand inside my dress, gently massaging my breast while we all watched the scene going on in front of us. My heart was beating fast, my eyes fixed on the couple writhing together on the couch as James leant in and kissed my neck while the woman played with my nipple, sending yet another shiver of pleasure through me.

Later we had moved back to the bar for a drink.

'Are you okay with this?' James asked.

'Are you kidding?' I replied, 'It's fabulous.'

Going back to the same room later, everything had changed and we stood for a moment, trying to make sense of what was happening in the gloom in front of us as limbs and buttocks moved around in a variety of combinations and clothing was unbuttoned and unzipped, material parted and slipped back.

'Can you work out what's happening?' James asked, leaning his lips so close to my ear that I could feel the warmth of his breath.

'Someone has their hand in my pussy,' I murmured.

Looking down, James lifted my skirt and revealed the elegant outline of a black man's hand sliding into my white panties. I leant in and kissed James's lips very gently as the fingers continued to massage me, creating a warm, silky wetness. The stranger's fingers were heightening the ecstasy I was experiencing in the same way as the toys we used at home. I realised that it was the young black guy we had been watching make love a few minutes before, and his elegant partner was standing on the other side, her arm round his waist, watching his hand working with the same level of interest as James was. I let out a whimper of pleasure. I had a stranger's hand in my panties and my boyfriend standing next to me watching it. I didn't even know the guy's name, but I didn't care.

Neither James nor I were sure how he would react to seeing another man fingering me like that, but he had relaxed so much, losing all the usual paranoia and jealousy which usually makes him follow me around clubs checking out any man who looks like he might be showing an interest. I know that it was not easy for him, that he was fighting with a mixture of excitement and jealousy. He liked that I was enjoying the attention but he knew without a doubt that he was the man I loved and the one I would be leaving and going home with.

The scenes we saw that night imprinted memories that I don't think will ever leave us, becoming images we would frequently conjure up when masturbating or when playing alone together and those scenes brought us back through the forbidding doors of the club many dozens of times in the coming years. It is games like this that are the most exciting and the most fun, the new experiences with a hint of promise of something more to experience later, such moments are sometimes even more sublime than the actual grunt and thrust of screwing.

The next morning I woke up in our sumptuous bed at Le Meurice to find myself lying safely in James's arms. He was holding me tight, breathing peacefully in my ear.

'What time is it?' I asked.

'I don't know.' He turned over and looked at the alarm clock. 'It's ten o'clock. You want some breakfast?'

'Oh yes, I'm starving.'

I called room service and placed my order, jumped out of bed, quickly going to the bathroom to brush my teeth before snuggling back under the huge duvet into James's arms again.

Still feeling sexy from the night before, we were soon kissing as passionately as if it was to be our last kiss ever. As we made love every touch and move felt more intense than ever. It felt as if we were in a different time zone. Just as we had managed to get our breathing back to normal the most delicious breakfast was discreetly delivered. Once I'd eaten all I could, I jumped out of bed and before

I could reach the huge marble bathroom I heard James pick up the phone.

'Good morning, Sir,' he said. 'Could you please try to get us a table for two at the Costes for one-thirty? Thank you. And please ask François down at the voiturier if he has a car available for me for a couple of hours.'

I couldn't stop smiling as I climbed into the shower and let the hot water cascade soothingly over my body. I was still shaky from the lovemaking and could feel James's cum running down between my legs. Once I had washed myself with the delicately scented soap, I patted my skin dry and chose a pair of brown tights, a denim mini-skirt with a cashmere turtleneck and brown suede high-heeled boots. Since we were going to have a driver, I knew there wasn't going to be too much walking and so I didn't need to worry about 'sensible' shoes. I could be totally indulgent. It was a chilly morning and I would need a coat but the sun was shining brightly outside the hotel windows and I couldn't wait to start the day. Happy with my choice and with my make-up and hair done I returned to the bedroom to find James was also ready to go.

'You look fantastic!' He said. 'I love your legs in that skirt.'

'Thank you.' As we left the room I felt like a million dollars.

'Let's go to Avenue Montaigne,' he suggested. 'We've got time before lunch.'

James told the driver to stop in front of the huge and impressive Gucci store. Going up to the women's floor I could already glimpse the new collection – such fabulous things. My hands were scrolling through the clothes but I'm always bad at choosing. James has a better eye for what suits me and when he's with me and in the mood to spoil me I let him do the selecting.

He asked for help and a pretty young lady picked out the right sizes for me, putting them in the changing cabin and leaving me to try on the first item, a black top with an elegant cleavage. It fitted perfectly. I came out of the cabin, still wearing my mini-skirt and I could see James loved it as he rolled his eyes and his mouth hung half open.

'We take that for sure,' he said. 'It's fantastic.'

Then I tried on a flowing black dress with long sleeves and a low neckline. It had a thin golden chain that hung over the waist. It was a very classy cut and super sexy, even though you couldn't see that much skin.

'Oh God,' James moaned when I came back out. 'We'll take that too. Love it!'

'I think it's a bit expensive,' I whispered, holding up two fingers to let him know it was two thousand euros.

'We still take it. It's too beautiful, you look amazing. You should wear that tonight if we go back to the club.'

Although James never even looks at the prices when he buys me gifts, I just can't bring myself to buy things when they are too expensive. It's just the way I am made and I know it is one of the things he loves about me.

'You need shoes, Penny,' he said, walking over to the shoe department, 'to go with the black dress.'

He held up a stunning pair of pumps with high golden heels. They were just made for the dress. I love shoes. I'm a total shoe freak. I'm obsessed with them. I'm like 'Carrie' in *Sex and the City*, which, incidentally is my favourite show! I don't care about handbags but shoes make me weak. I tried them on and they were just – wow!

James's eyes were sparkling as he gave them to the lady with a sign that we'd take them as well. I didn't dare even look at the price. Already I was imagining putting it all on that night to go back to the club. I definitely wanted to go back. It was so interesting and arousing. It was so much fun to discover this place with the man I loved and to be able to enjoy such unique experiences with him.

It took an age to have the stuff packed up and to finally pay. What is it with these big brand shops and their paying and wrapping methods? When we finally rushed out the driver loaded the bags into the boot, snapped it shut and we headed to our lunch reservation at the Costes, just five minutes away on rue du Faubourg Saint-Honoré.

I have grown to love the Costes and I'm an enormous fan of Jacques Garcia, the designer who took care of the entire remodelling and interior design. It's so classy with its use of different velvet fabrics, fireplaces and antique paintings. Every carpet and sofa is thought through in detail and the 'cour intérieure' is stunningly opulent.

James ordered a fantastic Lynch Bages, which was served in beautiful big glasses and we both ordered green lettuce salads. James followed that with Pasta à l'Arrabiata and I went for the Sole Meunière. Everything tasted like nectar. While we were eating we were dreaming and chatting about the night before, chewing over every delicious feeling and sensation we'd experienced, laughing at some of the scenes we had witnessed. We both needed to know if the other one had felt jealousy or fear, but neither of us had, apart perhaps from a tantalising fear of the unknown.

'It seems funny that I didn't feel jealous of any other woman whose ass I saw in there,' I mused.

'What is exciting,' James said, taking a thoughtful sip of wine, 'is to be "us" in that place. Going there to please anyone else would not make sense.'

We went on for hours analysing what had happened to us and what else might be out there in the big wide world that we had yet to discover. Once we had finished we grabbed a taxi, since James had sent the driver back to our hotel with the bags, and returned to the room for a long siesta, knowing that we intended to party again when we woke and would definitely be trying the club once more.

James had booked us in for dinner at Caviar Kaspia. We'd never been before but we had heard that it was the best place for caviar and Russian food. I thought it would be nice to have a tête à tête in a different place before going on afterwards to the club. When we woke up at seven thirty I ran a bath and started to prepare for the evening.

'Thank you again for all the wonderful things you bought me,' I said as I kissed James.

'Pleasure, Love. You look so beautiful in all of it.'

As I ran around unpacking my shopping I saw him typing on his iPhone.

'What are you doing?' I asked

'Nothing.'

'What, nothing? What are you typing then?'

'Just an SMS...'

I stopped asking questions. He had been sending messages quite often that day and I had a feeling that I shouldn't pry any further but that didn't stop me wondering. In the morning I had caught a glimpse of an incoming message but I hadn't recognised the name before he hurried off to the bathroom with the phone. What was going on?

The dinner was spectacular. We entered through a fish and caviar store and once upstairs there was a cosy atmosphere, amazing service and people sitting down for late dinners of caviar and salmon, washed down with iced vodka. I'm not a vodka fan, so we were more than happy to find a Baron de Ladoucette on the wine list. James made me taste three different caviars with a big baked potato. It was the best I had ever had and the first caviar I had ever eaten in a restaurant. In my family we would only open the caviar for special occasions, and always at home. My father would never have paid restaurant prices when he could get it from some good Persian friends at the best price. So for me as a kid caviar was only for Christmas or New Year. Having it served in a restaurant tête à tête was really special and I felt like a queen in my new dress and shoes, sharing this moment with the love of my life. I could see that he was just as happy as I was and enjoyed spoiling me. We both wanted to grasp every second we had together.

'What are you up to?' I asked.

'Why are you asking that?' he protested. 'I'm not up to anything.'

'What are your messages about? Anything new from the ex-wife's side?'

'No, not at all. I had the kids on the phone earlier. They're having a good time in Zermatt with her. They are taking the train back on Monday.'

'Yippee,' I said. 'Monday, back to reality. She'll start phoning again. When she's in town she needs to create stress.'

'Let's not talk about her tonight. Let's just enjoy. She'll ruin our evening otherwise and we don't want that.'

For the rest of the dinner we spoke about everything. I asked James a lot of questions and learned a lot about the world of law. It's so fascinating to listen to him and he has this way of making complex things understandable. He always loves to teach me his passions and I adore that about him. When we ordered the bill at midnight I didn't even dare to look at it.

'I feel really bad to have spent so much,' I said.

'It's a pleasure, Love. You deserve it and I love it when you appreciate things.'

As we came out of the restaurant our taxi was waiting.

I heard James giving the address to the driver and with a huge, excited grin I watched the Place Madeleine fading behind me.

This time we felt a lot more comfortable and emboldened about the whole scene when we arrived at the club. We had enjoyed several days of shopping, eating, relaxing and making love away from all the stresses and strains of home. We talked more easily with other people in the club than we had the first night, and danced with more abandon on the dancefloor. Going back behind the curtains again I lay down on a bed. James sat beside me and started to kiss me passionately, holding my face in his hands, his tongue exploring my lips until he noticed my eyes widen in surprise and pulled back to look down. A young Brazilian couple had joined us and were lying between my legs, alternately French kissing each other and licking my pussy. James gently lifted my head from the cushions so that I could watch what was happening in the candlelight at the same time as feeling their tongues flicking across me, teasing me, making me writhe with pleasure.

We spent hours wandering around the club that night, dancing, drinking, going in and out of the various rooms.

By the time we got back to our room at Le Meurice in the early hours of the morning we were like animals, both craving the flesh of the other, feasting as if we were starving, so high and excited by the adrenalin of our adventure together. I almost tore James's clothes off him I was so desperate to get to his dick, and it was so ready for me the moment it was free. All the images of the week, the smells, the sights, the music, the food, the wine and the ambience swirled together in our imaginations. He tasted so good and he was so hot and excited as we fought to consume every inch of each other's bodies.

The next morning our heads were a little heavy from so much good wine, and from the fact that we hadn't left the club till four thirty in the morning. It had been a great night but now it was time to go home. Our extended long weekend was ending and already we were feeling nostalgic for the times we had just had as we contemplated our return to the daily hassles of our lives. I didn't look forward to switching back from feeling like a romantic teenager again to being a parent, overseeing homework and enforcing bedtimes.

Our train back was in the afternoon so we had time to chill out in front of the television with a huge breakfast in bed. I love hotel breakfasts in bed. James seemed a little antsy and I got the feeling there was something he wasn't telling me.

'What is wrong with you?'

'Nothing,' he smiled and avoided my puzzled stare.

'Are you hiding something?'

'Not at all, all good...'

I started packing our suitcase and took a long hot bath before dressing and getting ready. James had our luggage picked up by the concierge and we headed downstairs.

'The hotel driver will take us to the station,' James told me.

'Great,' I replied, wondering why we just didn't get a cab since it was only a ten minute ride away.

After driving for about five minutes I didn't recognise the streets any more. This wasn't the route to the station. I looked at James and he smiled, squeezing my hand. Now I understood! The SMSs, the antsy attitude, the feeling he was hiding something...

Oh my God, he had rented a private jet to fly us back home. I couldn't believe it. That was the most exciting thing ever! I couldn't even sit still and try to look cool.

'You are crazy!'

'I know,' he grinned back, looking for all the world like a naughty little boy who has just done something delicious but forbidden.

When we arrived at Le Bourget a porter opened my door and I didn't see my luggage again until we arrived home. A hostess swept us into a lounge with huge leather sofas and offered us coffee and cookies. There was hardly any of the usual annoying airport business with metal detectors and x-ray machines and certainly none of the queuing, which can be so agitating when travelling. Ten minutes later we were strolling towards the waiting jet. The Captain welcomed us on the plush red carpet and introduced us to the co-pilot. Even the weather can't affect this wonderful courtesy; if it were raining he would still be waiting there with an umbrella.

Walking up those stairs and entering the quiet luxury of the plane, with its smooth wooden finishes and thick carpeting, I felt like a mega star. It was like stepping into the interior of a beautiful, spacious Bentley limousine. A plane all for ourselves! Amazing! As we sank into the soft leather seats I took James in my arms and hugged him as hard as I could.

Two minutes later the Captain was ready to go and before I could even get settled we were already going full speed down the runway and up into the sky. Wow! That was fast! Only minutes ago we were having breakfast in our bedroom at Le Meurice. It was like being beamed up into a private bubble amongst the clouds, sitting in a multi-million dollar machine. This was what real power felt like and it was so sexy. I was able to sit opposite James and open my legs just enough to give him a glimpse of my tiny white undies, knowing I was driving him nuts. I love it when he raises his eyes and slightly bites the inside of his cheek with pure desire. In fact the whole experience went too fast because I would happily have flown to Australia if it meant I could continue to enjoy the luxury of that cabin. It was so much fun. We were like two kids. The utmost luxury ever. I completely get why chief executives use private jets whenever they can. I think I'd trade pretty much anything for a trip in a private jet – apart of course from the man who made the whole thing possible!

CHAPTER THIRTEEN

Money was just never an issue between us. We certainly never fell out about it, but I was aware once things had settled down after the divorces that I needed to keep up with my own career so that I could start to build a college fund for Hannah, and to make sure that I could always pay for myself without ever having to ask James for money. I was also finding myself becoming a little bored without the stimulus of a job now that Hannah was at school for most of the day.

'I want to start my own company,' I said as we sat on in a restaurant after a meal.

'That sounds like a great idea,' James said, always the enthusiast, always positive. 'Can I be an investor?'

'No,' I said, knowing that he only wanted to invest because he believed in me. 'It's my baby! I don't want you involved in any way. It's enough to know you believe in me.'

'Okay,' he grinned and shrugged. 'Well, I definitely believe in you. Can I help with anything? A loan?'

'No, really, I'm just telling you what I'm planning, not asking for help.'

'That is one of the things that is really sexy about you,' he said, topping up my glass. 'You are never asking for anything, never giving me a hard time about money.'

'I don't need you in order to survive,' I said. 'I want to be with you because I love you.'

'I would love you to be my wife,' he said and I felt a warm glow of pleasure, mixed with a tiny stab of fear at the thought of everything that we had just escaped from with Frederic and Cecilia. 'But I'm afraid it would screw us up like it has screwed up everyone else we know.'

That was exactly how I felt. Once we were married would we start taking each other for granted, behaving like everyone else does once they know the other person 'belongs' to them?

'Ask me when I'm sixty,' I grinned. 'If you still love me then, and still like my ass as much, then I'll say yes.'

He nodded and smiled back. 'Anyway,' he said, 'I'm not leaving this world without you being my wife. I just want you to know that. Okay, so tell me what you want to do and how.'

'Well, I'm good with event management and I think I could make a business out of it. I could organise weddings, for example, or dinner parties, bar mitzvahs, marketing events, all that sort of thing.'

'It sounds like a great idea and with the network we have I could help you find a lot of clients. You can help me out sometimes with my clients.'

For the rest of the night we discussed my strategies, chose a company name and worked out how to get started. At about three in the morning we were toasting the launch of my new venture. It was so much fun having James encouraging me and believing in what I was capable of and backing me in every way except financially. That part I needed to do myself. I needed to keep that part separate. Within a week I had set up a logo, printed my business cards, met with a lawyer to set up the company and organised my office from home. I also called a designer friend, who helped me create a webpage. Within a fortnight I was up and running.

Now I needed clients. The first one came through James's uncle, whose friend wanted to throw a cocktail party for a financial presentation at the Principe Leopoldo Hotel. From that first commission word of mouth spread and other jobs followed. What had started as merely being something to occupy my spare hours became hectic and I had to hire a freelance accountant to handle the books for me. I was loving everything about it and it left me free to organise my own schedules in coordination with both James and Hannah. Our life as a couple, and my role as a mother, were still my priorities but I believe it is important that my daughter sees a working mom and I know that she is very proud of me and understands that the money I earn is for her education.

It's not easy to hold down a job, take care of a child and live a fulfilled relationship, but for me it works. In order to be a happy mother I need to be a fulfilled woman, and that is exactly what I am.

* * * * * *

'Why don't we order someone to the room?' I suggested, 'rather than going back out there.'

We were in Shanghai for James's business. We'd been excited about going there because we'd heard how new and vibrant and exciting the whole city was. We love Hong Kong and we imagined Shanghai would provide us with the same sort of experience, but maybe even better. It was certainly a booming and exciting city, growing and spreading at an incredible rate, a fabulous lightshow at night and a buzzing hive of activity twenty-four hours a day, the streets filled with rushing, spitting crowds of people, the towering buildings constantly growing in their cocoons of fragile-looking bamboo scaffolding. In fact the whole experience was so huge we felt completely overwhelmed and disconcertingly out of our comfort zone. I was hyper with excitement, jumping around like an excited child.

It was alarming not be able to talk to the taxi drivers. We rely a lot on taxi drivers when we're in unfamiliar cities and it's always the most dangerous, and exciting, moment of any night out, the moment when we reveal that we're strangers in town and that we're relying on them for information and trusting them not to take advantage of us. It usually takes us a few bottles of wine and many hours of discussion to pluck up the courage to take these plunges into the unknown. You never know what sort of communities a cab driver might come from and whether they will be taking you to a part of the city that could be dangerous. James always works on the premise of being really friendly and really generous, and he then pays them to wait outside the place for us, so that we always have an escape car ready, should anything go wrong. We don't want to find ourselves trapped in a difficult situation in a place we don't know, with no means of transport.

The main thing we both want when we are alone together anywhere is to have fun. We try hard to be good and sensible and get to bed early and not get into trouble, but we always end up dissolving into giggles and giving in to the temptation to go looking for adventure. Sometimes we might have been travelling for twenty hours, jet-lagged and desperately in need of rest, but we just can't resist looking for something fun to do. The sensible sides to our natures tell us to wait, to slow down – but why wait? We lay plans to go see the museums and the other sights the next day and then we start laughing because we know that even if we do all those things we still won't be getting an early night first. So many people spend their whole lives waiting just because they don't dare to suggest doing something a little bit daring. One of the things I admire most in James is the fact that he is always daring to ask, no matter how outrageous the idea might be and no matter how long it might take him to pluck up the courage in the first place.

Shanghai looked so exciting we wanted to do something fun but we didn't know where to start. Between us we speak six languages fluently but in Shanghai we found ourselves unable to communicate with anyone outside the hotel, which left us feeling frustrated and vulnerable. Even James found it impossible to work his charms on the local population. The Peninsula Hotel was just as fantastic as it is in Hong Kong, but every time we stepped beyond its doors the city drenched us in noise, dust and bewilderment.

That was how we came to find ourselves wide awake with jet lag that night, having had a massage and come up to the room with the intention of getting an early night, not wanting to venture outside the calm comfort of the hotel, and decided to look for someone to distract us.

'Okay,' James said. 'I'm game for that. If it doesn't work out, just having another massage would be nice.'

We went online and found a number to ring. It was impossible to tell if the woman James was speaking to fully understood what we wanted, or whether she was just saying whatever she thought we wanted to hear. By the time he hung up we still had no idea whether the wrong sort of person would turn up at the bedroom door. If it had been someone bad we would have just thanked her, paid her and James would have told her I was not feeling well. We waited with mounting excitement, straining our ears for the sound of approaching footsteps.

The little Chinese girl who tapped lightly on our bedroom door an hour or so later, however, arrived as silently as a morning mist, and was unbelievably cute. She was a sweet, delicate, oriental beauty. This was a huge bonus. For us 'pretty' is not as important as 'fun'. We always want to find people who will enjoy playing around as much as we will. This girl seemed to be both pretty and fun.

James explained as best he could through the language barrier that she was there to massage me, so she didn't have to fear him, but her eyes were calm and showed no sign of anxiety.

'This is for the agency,' he said, giving her the agreed amount, 'and this is just for you.' He gave her the same amount again. We are always meticulous about this sort of thing because we know that however nice we might be to them, prostitutes would nearly always prefer not to have to do the things they do. We will never try to force them to do anything because it would be no fun for us if they were not having fun, and we want to make very sure they are extremely well compensated financially for even being there at all. James is always meticulous in treating them with respect, wanting to make them feel safe and valued and confident enough to say if there is anything they do or don't want to do. He is never interested in penetrating other women and he lets them know immediately that they have nothing to fear as far as he is concerned.

He then suggested that I undress and lie on my front on the bed and asked the girl if she would like to massage me. I was happy to let him take control of the situation, just wanting to relax and be pampered, and already feeling the familiar, pleasant ache of anticipation rippling through me.

Nodding happily, she took a bottle of baby oil from her bag and placed it carefully on the side before going into the bathroom to shower. As she walked back into the room she was unselfconsciously patting her flawless skin with a thick, fluffy hotel towel, making no attempt to cover her nakedness. It was the most perfect little body I had ever seen, like a painting.

Once she had dried herself she climbed naked on top of me, straddling my buttocks as if mounting a horse, light as a feather, the skin on her inner thighs as soft and cool as silk. I felt the gentle pressure of dainty, oiled fingers running from my neck to the small of my back and the insides of her smooth thighs moving back and forth against my skin. After several minutes of massaging my back and shoulders she slid onto the bed beside me and her tiny fingers caressed the oil into my buttocks, sliding down between my cheeks, slipping into every crevice, exploring and teasing. I relaxed, parting my thighs to allow her better access, confident now that she understood perfectly what we wanted, needing to feel her touching and entering my sex.

James had also undressed while he watched us and after a few moments he climbed onto the bed beside her. I became hungry for more pleasure, desperate to go higher. I turned onto my back and parted my legs wide so that both he and the girl could take turns licking me, pampering me, making me moan and writhe until I eventually came with a delicious shiver of relief. James rolled onto his back and I climbed on top of him, slipping his erection easily inside me and moving it in the way I know he likes, stroking him between the tops of his legs and up across his thighs and trembling stomach while the girl knelt behind me, continuing to caress my back and my breasts, my thighs and my ass.

Once James had exploded inside me we told our guest she could stop. Climbing off the bed with a sweet smile and a polite bow, she padded back into the bathroom, leaving the door open. We lay together, our energies spent, listening to the sound of the bath tub being filled. After a few minutes I stood up and went to see what she was doing.

'Come and look,' I whispered to James and he came to stand beside me in the doorway. She was sitting with perfect, upright posture in the middle of the gigantic bathtub, carefully washing herself with the hand shower and soap with only the light from the bedroom illuminating the peaceful, beautiful scene.

As she left, very reluctantly, which made us feel good because we could see we had made her feel very comfortable being with us in the room, James asked for her private telephone number. She seemed very happy when we rang her again the following night and asked her to join us in the room again. We'd been thinking and talking about her all day and wanted to spend more time with her before we left Shanghai, hopefully forever. She was so perfectly beautiful to look at and knew exactly how to please me I wanted to take time and drink my fill of her company.

When she arrived at the room we all felt far more relaxed than the previous night, as if welcoming back an old friend. We started as we had the first time with her massaging and stimulating me while James took off his clothes and joined us on the bed. This time, however, I came very quickly since we had been working ourselves up to a high point of anticipation by talking about our new friend all day. James could feel me shudder and then relax from my climax, continuing to enjoy the girl's soothing caresses. I felt so satisfied and comfortable I wanted to do something else for James, something that would be interesting for me too. After a few minutes I put my hand on the back of the girl's head, feeling the softness of her glossy black hair, and gently guided her sweet face down until her parted rosebud lips softly received the tip of his erection. She happily started to taste him with tiny flicks of her tongue. Confident that I didn't mind, he lay back to enjoy the sensation and after watching for a moment or two I slipped off the bed and went into the bathroom, leaving them alone while I took a shower.

Once I'd had my shower I came back into the room and stood watching the perfect curves of this elegant little body kneeling between his legs, her head bobbing gently up and down as she pleasured him.

After watching them for a while I sat back down on the bed and kissed James, our tongues entwining as the girl continued teasing his penis with her lips and tongue, then I put my hand on her shoulder. She raised her head from James's erection, allowing me to climb on top of him and guide him inside me while the girl curled up under the covers beside us, stroking us and allowing us to stroke her as we both came to a climax together.

When it was all over James and I drifted towards sleep while the girl stayed quietly beside us in the bed. I guess she was in no hurry to get dressed and go back outside into the ugly world of the Shanghai slums that I imagine she came from, and we were in no hurry to break the spell either. It was nice to have met someone who was so beautiful and so much fun to be with.

* * * * * *

The following night we ventured out to the French Concession Area for dinner, a place just for 'ex-pats'. The food was not great at all, but for us as business people it was extremely interesting just to experience the sheer volume of what was happening in the city that was now housing twenty-three million people and still growing.

When we got back to the room the in-house channel was playing a movie about the Kadorie family, the Iraqi-Jewish family that settled in Hong Kong and developed the Peninsular Group of hotels that can now be found all over South East Asia as well as places like New York and Los Angeles. The movie was showing the changes that have happened to Shanghai over the last hundred years. It was a shock to see what was little more than a sprawling shanty town growing a high-tech skyline to rival any in the world. The city's story actually made us feel quite emotional.

There's something charming about the 'good old days' of the British Empire, which is what makes Hong Kong so cool, but something exciting at the same time about the pace with which everything is now moving forward in the Far East. I love the British structure and discipline that underlies the whole thing, but the raw, swelling power of mainland China is exciting too and since handover Hong Kong has become their playground as well.

Leaving the city the next day on the new seven-lane highway which was already crowded with cars, we looked back and saw the mist of dirt hanging over the fascinating, pulsating skyline. The ultra-modern airport was fabulous, serving us with the best dumplings ever as we sat in front of the most fantastic, futuristic, 3D high-definition screens like nothing we had ever seen before. There were planes departing constantly, linking Shanghai to every thriving destination in the world. In the sumptuous comfort of Cathay Pacific Business Class James could watch golf on the in-flight program while I slept the sleep of the angels, still as exhausted and jet-lagged as the day we arrived, but content that we had squeezed every ounce of fun we could have from our few days in this new, amazing and dazzling city.

Whenever we visit somewhere new we always speculate as to whether we could actually live there. In the case of Shanghai the answer was definitely 'no', but what a blast it was to see the place at the moment when it was emerging from its ancient chrysalis into the modern world.

* * * * * *

'I've heard that in this city you can get someone to come to your room within ten minutes,' I said. 'It would be fun to test that out, wouldn't it?'

'Sure,' James said, opening his computer, ready to take the plunge if I was.

After suffering the culture shock of Shanghai we had returned to Hong Kong like fish being dropped back into water, both of us so relieved to be in a city we knew well and had enjoyed so much in the past. We were in the Peninsula Hotel in Kowloon.

Once James had found a website we pored over it for hours, as usual, before plucking up the courage to make the call, discussing all the various options before deciding to try something new and ordering a couple: a guy and a woman. It was a very different potential situation to just hiring one person, far more fraught with possibilities, and also with possible dangers. By the time James hung up the phone the tension had tightened every muscle and nerve in my body. We'd set the ball rolling, but there was still time to call it off if our courage deserted us. The minutes ticked by and still we hadn't decided whether we would actually be able to go through with it. The phone rang, making us jump. James picked up, listened, said something affirmative and hung up.

'They're in reception,' he said, 'but I've got to go down and negotiate with the concierge because there's a house rule that staff shouldn't let other people up to the rooms after midnight without them being signed in by a guest.'

It was alright for me, I could hide in the room, but James was going to have to step out and expose himself in the marbled vastness of the virtually empty night-time lobby, the giant potted palms providing scant cover. There was no option. Even if he chickened out, paid them and sent them away he still had to go down to the lobby in order to do so. We both made a conscious effort to control our breathing and then he went out to the lift.

The couple were waiting discreetly in the huge, hushed lobby. The concierge's face was entirely impassive as James emerged from the lift and walked over to them. He was not going to make James's life unnecessarily difficult, he was too well trained for that. James forced his doubts aside and took the plunge, acting as naturally as possible. Before they could come up he had to agree to put their names on his ID. The thing he hated most was that the guy behind the desk didn't know that I was involved, that I was upstairs waiting. He undoubtedly thought James was doing something behind my back and James didn't like that, but there was nothing he could say that wouldn't have made things seem even worse.

They were a cute couple, her with a fake Gucci bag and a fake Gucci cap. They seemed like they were a couple themselves, although we couldn't be sure. Certainly they seemed to know each other well. They talked for a while in the lobby. James took care of the money side, signed in with the concierge and then headed back to the lifts with them.

I liked the look of them from the moment they came into the room and James introduced them. When they entered the palatial white bathroom we could hear a lot of giggling going on. James was being a little more specific in his requests than usual. He wanted to be sure we stayed in control of everything that happened, aware that they might have drugs on them and not wanting to risk being caught up in any sort of embarrassing police sting.

By the time they came out all four of us were naked. They were very uninhibited and both had nice bodies. The girl and I started by taking turns tasting James.

'Do you want to lick her ass?' James asked the guy and he readily agreed. What we didn't realise was that the guy would not take any initiative himself and would simply keep following instructions until we told him to stop. James became distracted by what the girl and I were doing to him, engrossed in watching our faces taking turns to lick him.

'Is he still licking you?' he asked eventually.

'Yes,' I sighed happily.

'It must have been fifteen minutes!'

'I know!'

'Who does that?' he asked and I could feel him shaking in his attempt to control the laughter bubbling up from deep inside him.

I shrugged, knowing that memories of this moment were going to be making us both giggle for a long time.

'It's okay now,' James told him, forcing himself not to laugh for fear of offending him, and the poor guy came up like a deep sea diver, gratefully filling his lungs with fresh air.

* * * * * *

Driving up to the Victoria Peak in Hong Kong provides one of the greatest contrasts in the world, leaving the buildings that seem from the ground to stretch up to the skies, and actually being able to look down on them from above. Steel and concrete are suddenly replaced by jade green trees and fresh clear air even on one of the most crowded and urbanised islands on Earth. The air was misty and damp and as we climbed out of the car James told the driver he could go and we would find our own way down.

Even though I didn't think he had any more idea how to get down the mountain than I did, I still felt completely safe with him, as I always do. James always knows what he is doing and can always find his way anywhere. He only has to glance at a map and he is able to memorise it. He simply never gets lost, having a sense of direction that is almost freaky.

The mist was becoming a fog as we went to the viewing point and looked down at the sea of cloud below, unable to see anything of the famous harbour.

'Great view, no?' James said, straight-faced, and we both dissolved into giggles.

We found our way to the deserted funicular, unchanged since colonial times, and sat holding one another as we descended, kissing passionately as we rumbled back down past the beautiful, modern emblematic Bank of China building, back onto the bustle and glitter of the city streets.

* * * * * *

We have always made a promise to ourselves that we will never stop ourselves from 'going the extra mile' in pursuit of having fun. We never want to fall into the trap of curtailing a night out prematurely just because we 'have to be up in the morning'. We have seen so many of our friends' relationships shrivelling on the vine because they are so concerned about getting home to bed. Sometimes, of course, that means we have to operate at work or on the school run after only one or two hours' sleep a night, but we're certain the sacrifice is worth it. We'll have plenty of time to sleep when we're dead.

We have, however, made one exception to that rule, which is that we should try to get at least a few hours' sleep if we are booked onto a long-haul flight the following morning. We agreed on this rule after having made ourselves feel very ill on several occasions by changing time zones and adding jet lag to a general lack of sleep.

That was how we found ourselves in our room on the last night of our stay in Hong Kong. We'd enjoyed a long dinner and taken the lift back to our room like good little children. Our cases were all packed and everything was done in preparation to leave, but now neither of us was feeling tired. James took out his laptop and started playing around. We both kept reminding each other that we 'should' go to sleep, but then we would decide that maybe we could just look at 'one more thing' on the screen. We were both having too much fun in each other's company to want to end it, like little children too excited to want to give in to sleep, however tired they might be.

We brought up an agency website and we were looking at pictures of girls, and still we weren't tired. The idea of going to sleep just didn't seem as interesting as trying to provoke a bit of fun. I find it cute that James still feels shy about suggesting things sometimes, even though neither of us feels any shame about sharing our fantasies with one another, knowing neither of us will ever judge the other. But still he is a little shy and that is very sexy.

We knew we 'should' just close the computer and go to bed but now we were starting to feel extremely sexy and we didn't want to waste our last few hours in Hong Kong lying in bed, staring into the dark and trying to go to sleep. We started to compare and discuss the different girls and then a blonde came up on the screen. She looked like she might be a Russian, and in our experience Russian women are not always the most fun people, but I made an instant decision anyway.

'Phone that one,' I said. 'And then order us something to eat because I'm hungry again.'

When she knocked at the bedroom door a few minutes after the phone call James felt suddenly nervous and asked me to let her in. I gave him what I hoped was a withering look and put down the Club Sandwich I was attacking with relish, picking out the bacon and nibbling it separately as I always do, which for some reason James finds hysterical. When I opened the door I was surprised to find two women outside. One was a brown-haired girl who looked nothing like the picture, and the other was an older woman. Both were Russian and I immediately had a foreboding that we might have made a mistake. Neither of them exactly looked like they were fun people.

'Who are you?' I asked the older woman.

'I am just here to introduce her and make sure she's okay,' she said in broken English.

'Come in,' I shrugged and ushered them in before going back to my sandwich. 'Are we doing the old lady too?' I hissed at James out of the corner of my mouth as I chewed. 'Who is she?'

'Maybe she's her mother,' James hissed back and I tried to stifle the beginnings of a giggling fit with my napkin.

After a few minutes of painful small talk the old woman obviously decided we looked harmless enough and left. The girl sat frozen and glum, apparently expecting something to happen. I continued chewing and looking at her curiously, waiting for James to sort something out. He seemed nonplussed.

'Have you always had brown hair?' I broke the silence.

'No,' the girl replied, 'I changed it just two days ago.'

'Do you want a drink?'

'I'll have a beer.'

We gave her a beer and the poor girl continued to sit there, not knowing what to do next. James pulled himself together and sorted out the money, but that made her look even more lost and unsure what was expected of her.

'How long have you been in Hong Kong?' I enquired.

'I just arrived two days ago.'

I looked at James with one eyebrow raised, trying to suppress the giggles I could feel bubbling up.

'What do I have to do now?' the girl asked.

'Don't worry about it,' I said. 'Let's just see what happens.'

'I don't do women,' she said quickly.

We exchanged looks again. It looked like we might have problems because she definitely wasn't there to 'do' James. That was never why he hired girls. She was there to create something for both of us.

'If you need the bathroom,' James said to the girl, trying to ease the atmosphere, 'just help yourself.'

She disappeared into the bathroom while I finished my sandwich, undressed and climbed onto the bed. The girl came out and perched on the edge. She had a good body, beautiful breasts and her ass was perfect. When she finally cracked a smile she was actually quite pretty, not that that was important, but somehow she still didn't look like she was having much fun.

'What do I do now?' she asked.

'Just relax,' James said. He started kissing my neck the way I love, then my lips and then down to my breasts. Opening my eyes for a second I saw the girl kneeling at the end of the bed just staring at us. We didn't want to push her to do anything if she didn't want to. We wouldn't even have minded if she had just taken the money and left because it would have made us laugh.

The girl looked at my naked body and looked back at James. 'You don't tell anybody I do another woman,' she said, 'or I lose my reputation.'

Neither of us dared catch the other's eye. She was Russian. We were western European. We were all in Hong Kong. We didn't know her real name and she didn't know ours. Who exactly did she think we were going to tell and what reputation was she frightened of losing exactly?

Seeing that she now felt safe, James took the initiative, guiding her head down towards my intimate parts. Finally she seemed to get the idea that it might be fun to play along, but things were not going smoothly and I hit my head on the end of the bed, which made the mood even more awkward. She was very clumsy and not even bothering to fake any passion. I explored her body a little, but her pussy was not attractive and I wasn't getting very turned on by any of it.

'Forget it,' I whispered into James's ear, 'she doesn't want to be here.'

'I know,' he said, 'but we can still have fun anyway.'

He thought there was still a chance we could transform the scene into something sexy and so he lay on his back and I climbed on top of him, sliding him inside me with such ease. I loved taking James, and being taken by him like that. There were three naked people in the bed and the love of my life inside me. It was very hot despite everything. With his left arm around my back he hugged me to him, my tits so tight against his wonderful chest I could feel his heart beating. The girl was hovering around uncertainly and James gently pulled my left buttock cheek aside.

'Do you want to lick her?' he asked politely. She sighed deeply and went to work.

By five in the morning, with our plane due to leave at eight, we finally gave up on trying to make the night interesting and the girl left, still begging us not to tell any of her friends what she had done that night. We had one hour in which to sleep before we had to be up and ready to stumble into one of the hotel's famous fleet of green Rolls-Royces to go to the airport.

It was a lesson to us: we should have gone to bed like good children in the first place, but we both knew we would be making the same mistake again because you never know, next time it just might turn out to be a really good experience.

When we got to the airport we were queuing for the X-ray and a toddler in front of us had made a puddle on the floor. As we waited for our bags we watched his parents as they struggled to clean it up and exchanged looks, both of us wanting to giggle at this contrast to what we had been doing over the previous few nights and aware that we too were now on our way back to the real world. James wanted to go shopping before we boarded our flight but I had finally reached the end of my energy levels, hiding my aching eyes behind large sunglasses.

'I'm going to the first-class lounge,' I told him, 'to sit down and have some dim sum.'

I could see he was fighting the urge to laugh as he followed me onto the escalator, which was crammed full of other travellers. Halfway up I whipped off my dark glasses and turned back to him.

'I have just one thing to say,' I announced to the entire escalator, 'I am done with Russian putains.'

With that I slammed my glasses back over my eyes and continued on my stately way to the top, aware that James was simultaneously blushing and laughing behind me. From now on I was determined to concentrate on people who got as much fun out of life as we did.

Whenever we return home from our trips together, whether they are long or short, it is always a hard landing. We both have our work to worry about and I have my childcare duties and we have to leave behind the carefree, youthful behaviour that we are able to indulge in when it is just us, but it doesn't take long to get back into the rhythm of our lives, going to our favourite restaurants, spending happy hours reminiscing about our latest adventures, enjoying them all over again, constantly saying 'can you believe that was us that did that?' The sexiest part of having experimented with something new and fun and daring is thinking and talking about it afterwards when it is just the two of us together in our own bed again, making love in the ways we have always loved the best.

CHAPTER FOURTEEN

'Penny, I have to show you something,' James said, appearing from nowhere in the mirror behind me in the hairdressing salon in Zurich, where I was having a brushing done for a birthday party we had been invited to.

'What is it?'

'I'll show you when you're finished here.'

Now that he had piqued my curiosity I started to feel impatient with the poor girl as she continued to fiddle with my hair, anxious to find out what he wanted me to see so badly. When she was finally satisfied we paid and he hurried me out into the street, pulling on my arm like an excited little boy and pushing me into a nearby shop.

'I hate golf,' I protested, looking round the huge display area, 'what do you want me to do in here?'

'Just have a look around,' he said, 'It's such cool stuff.'

Rolling my eyes, I trailed along behind him, looking at hundreds of different golfing products. I knew he had been hooked on the sport before his marriage and had had to give it up because it was impossible to play with Cecilia on his back all the time and young babies at home. I could all too easily imagine the crisis he would have had to go through if he was to leave the house for eighteen holes of golf on a Sunday morning, while she was breastfeeding or pushing the kids in a stroller to the park.

Personally I had never been fond of the game. I had never had a club in my hands and didn't even know what a putter was for. I'd watched it on television occasionally and thought it was the most boring thing in the world. Most probably because I didn't understand a thing about it and I am the biggest anti-sport person ever. Going to the gym for me is about as appealing as going to the dentist and I am bad skier, I can hardly even sit on a bike.

'Just look at this stuff,' James was enthusing as he went from one display to the next. 'Just have a look around. I have never seen such a huge golfing shop before.'

I had to admit he was starting to catch my interest as we looked through the nice clothes, the golf shoes, bags and other accessories. I began to see how classy it all was. Going further into the back of the shop we came to the golf club section. There were bags in every colour and each set of clubs seemed nicer than the last. I started to take a note of their names; Callaway, Taylormade, Ping...

'How does anyone know which brand to choose?' I asked. 'And how do you choose which clubs?'

'You have to like the looks,' he explained. 'You have to like the sensation of them in your hands and feel comfortable with them.'

Intrigued, I picked up a set of clubs I liked the look of and stared at a magnificent golf bag.

'Let's buy you everything you need,' he said, 'and you can give it a try.'

'And if I don't like it?'

'Then we can sell the clubs and the rest we don't care about.'

My reluctance was melting away. It was starting to be a very cool afternoon. Two hours later I walked out of there with a set of clubs, a golf bag, shoes, balls, gloves and a travel bag. As usual James had managed to sweep me along on a wave of enthusiasm.

'You sure know how to get a girl hooked,' I grinned, giving him a peck on the cheek and snuggling up close. 'You are crazy.'

Back in our room at the Hyatt we practised our putting into an up-turned garbage bin and I found I was having a blast.

'I'll arrange for you to have a lesson on Monday,' James said, 'and you can check out if you like it.'

To my amazement I loved it and we started going to the range together around three times a week. I got into my lessons big time because I now wanted to pass my test in order to be able to go onto the course. I learned very fast and in mid-November, in temperatures of three degrees and thick fog, I passed. Since that moment in the shop in Zurich, golf has become a passion and a major part of our life together and I am truly grateful to James for knowing how to make it interesting. I am so lucky to have a guy who encourages me on the course without wanting to teach me or criticise whenever I miss a shot. I have played with so many couples where the poor wives have to listen to a constant stream of derogatory remarks about their playing. We became members at the magnificent Lugano Golf Club and we are often to be found in the bar having imbibed too much wine after we have finished the eighteenth hole together, unable to stop talking about every shot.

* * * * * *

I love to join James for business lunches, partly because I just want to be with him and listen to him talking, but also because I find I can hold my own in any conversation with any of his clients and I know that excites him. Being together like that, around a table with other people, feeling the bond between us that is still as strong as the days when we were at school together, is always so sexy. It makes the adrenalin pump.

'You know what?' James said, once his clients had left the restaurant after a particularly long and stimulating lunch, 'I've always wanted to go to a real porn movie. I've walked past the theatres a million times but I've never plucked up the courage to go in.'

'That is so low life,' I laughed at the naughty look on his face. I could see that he had had to pluck up all his courage to even mention such a thing, and he could see that my curiosity had been roused by the thought of venturing into this new forbidden territory. What exactly did happen inside those threatening-looking places? Would it be fun to find out? Did we have the nerve to try? After an hour or so of thinking and talking about it, and a few more glasses of wine, we were ready to take the plunge.

'You know,' he whispered as we got close to the entrance, 'I would never have the nerve to go into a place like this on my own.'

'This is going to be such fun,' I said, squeezing his arm, keeping up my own courage as much as his, 'and really interesting.'

The theatre was just as sleazy as you would imagine, the seats dotted with men, about twenty of them. There were two films showing at once, one upstairs on the balcony, the other downstairs. We managed to position ourselves in two seats on the side so we could see both screens, and keep our eyes on the other customers at the same time. It was very sexy, partly because I could tell that this was not a safe place for me to be. All our senses were on high alert and my heart was beating hard. I had seen porn movies in the past where they use the plot device where a man brings a woman into an auditorium, just like this one, and the other men there start to approach her. It inevitably ends as an orgy scene with one woman amongst a whole bunch of men, which was not an attractive prospect.

It seemed more than likely that all these men had seen the same scenes played out on screens, and no doubt in their imaginations as well. When they saw me appear through the curtains into the darkened auditorium, my face sporadically illuminated by the flickering light from the screens, they must have thought all their wildest fantasies had just come true. Once my eyes had adjusted to the dark I could see that several of them were now looking in our direction, like a pack of hyenas spotting an antelope wandering innocently into their territory, shooting me sidelong glances, biding their time until they had plucked up the courage to move closer.

Despite everything I was still turned on by the whole scene, the noises of lovemaking from the screen and the impending danger all around us. I slid my fingers up under my skirt to play with myself. There was a sudden bang in the dark as a seat sprang up and a man moved through the gloom to sit next to me on the other side. He leant in, breathing heavily, and mumbled a suggestion that we should have a threesome. I could feel all the other men's eyes on us now, assessing what was going to happen next and wondering whether there would be any morsels in it for them.

At that moment James decided things were in danger of getting out of his control. He grabbed my hand and we made a dash for the exit, both panting and giggling like naughty school children once we were safely back in the light and running through familiar streets.

CHAPTER FIFTEEN

My divorce arrangement stipulated that I could stay a couple of years in the flat that Frederic and I had bought before we separated. It was a relief to have that opportunity, even though it led to a lot of fights with Frederic. It gave me a roof over my head and a breathing space in which to reorganise my life without having to move again right away, which would have put Hannah through another trauma.

After living there for two years with James, however, it started to feel uncomfortable to be in a flat that was initially Frederic's, although James was always happy to contribute to the costs of the household, including the maid's salary and all the bills. It was time to find a place of our own and to make a fresh start between walls of our own choosing. We did not, however, intend to go about it in the way that most couples choose their houses together.

First of all a house was not an option. We were not the types for a little garden and a pool. Our needs were very specific. We wanted a flat in the countryside outside Lugano in order to be a little way away from town and from Cecilia. It also felt important that there were bedrooms for James's children to come to on their weekends with their dad.

James didn't want to be involved in the search, which doubled the fun for both of us.

'Penny,' he said when we discussed it, 'I came to your flat to live with you and it was all great and just fine and I loved it. This time should be the same and you should choose the place, decorate it and do the moving and when it's ready I'll come. It's your home and I want it to be the same way it has been for the last two years. This way there are no conflicts and we don't have to do all that "couple" shit of having to choose furniture together on a Saturday afternoon.'

'This sounds awesome,' I said.

So we discussed the budget and I then started my flat hunting in the areas I liked.

I went onto different real estate websites for rentals and took about ten meetings for visits. I love searching flats and visiting and I'm not the kind of person who needs to think a hundred times about every decision. But for the first two weeks I only saw horrible stuff for huge budgets. I kept in mind how we would fit into the rooms and how the flats were arranged. I wanted the maximum privacy for everyone and the maximum practicality. For two months I searched but nothing came up.

Beginning to wonder if I would ever find the right place, I went back to surfing the web and spotted a flat that had been totally redone so that it looked like a little townhouse in a village thirty minutes from Lugano. I had a good feeling as I picked up the phone and dialled the number.

When the landlord opened the door to me I knew I had found our new home. It was perfect. Six bedrooms on different floors, all very well laid out and spacious. Everything was newly done and the rent was less than our maximum budget.

'I found it,' I SMSd James right away.

A second later my phone beeped. 'Take it!' he replied.

'I'll take it,' I told the landlord. 'When can we move in?'

'Done,' I messaged back to James a few minutes later. 'We're moving in next month.'

Over the next four weeks I put carpets in the bedrooms and painted the walls in warm colours. I need colours, I can't live in white. I also needed to buy furniture for James's kids and a new bed for us. It was a huge excitement. My own flat with James. A new home for our new life. It was more than I could ever have dreamed of. I couldn't believe that it was finally 'us' after all that suffering during all those years. Now we had our own home, only us. It was a dream come true. We were both so happy and James was becoming incredibly excited at the prospect of finding out what I had arranged for us.

On the day of the move James was busy at work and that night he went to a hotel with his kids as he had them that Friday and I had my hands full with the move. I wanted it all to be ready for him to see the next morning. I am extremely efficient in moving and in general I can make a place feel like home right away. I never do the 'living out of boxes for months' thing.

Hannah was ecstatic, helping everywhere, getting her toys stored away in her new home. It meant a lot to her. She was getting a sense of security back, something she had lost after the separation and it meant that James was there now. She would be going to her new school after the summer so it was a new start for her in many ways.

That night I spent alone in the flat with Hannah and our maid and I could hardly sleep from the excitement, wondering if James would love it and if he would be as happy as I was. The next morning he arrived. I opened the door and jumped around his neck, I was so happy and I immediately saw he was feeling the same way.

'Welcome home,' I smiled. 'Let me show you around.'

Room by room he discovered his new home and was amazed by everything he saw. He *loved* it. He was as excited as a small boy. I explained what needed to be added and what was still to be delivered and he just kept nodding and grinning and staring around him in wonder.

Standing in the living room he put his arms around me. 'Penny,' he said, 'you are the best. I love this place and what you have done with it and all your work. You are amazing.'

'I am really looking forward to inaugurating our new bed,' I said.

'Me too.'

That night we made love like two birds who had just found the keys to happiness and freedom. We held each other tight all night long and it all felt so perfect, so right.

* * * * * *

'Hiring someone to come to an anonymous hotel room in a foreign city is very different to having someone come to your own home,' I said as we sat sipping a great Gavi di Gavi with piccata al limone just round the corner from our apartment. It had been a particularly boring weekend, filled with parental chores, and we were both relieved to finally be alone together and able to talk about grown up things.

'True,' he said. 'Wouldn't it be sexy and fun, though?'

'It might be,' I agreed, already warming to the idea. Talking about new things, trying out different ideas, exploring possibilities, laying possible plans, is often the sexiest and most fun part of any adventure.

The conversation went back and forth for several hours, one minute one of us getting nervous, the next moment the other, before James took out his iPad and found a site where you could hire people in the Lugano area for this type of service.

We still hadn't made a final decision by the time we got home and I had opened us another bottle of wine. We must have spent another two hours happily browsing the site, looking at pictures, comparing them, wondering if we dared to make the phone call or not. Our hearts were beating in anticipation of a new adventure, something different, possibly dangerous, possibly embarrassing, but maybe fabulous. We looked through the women first.

'What about a guy?' he suggested.

I was trying to work out exactly what was going through his head. Was he testing me? If I said 'yes' would he want to know why the hell I would need someone else?

'Would you be okay with that?' I asked.

'If I guide you,' he said, 'and have total control of the situation, then yes, I am okay with it. Actually I find the idea quite exciting.'

I guess many women would like the idea of two men taking care of them simultaneously, but it took a lot of nerve to actually say 'let's do it'. I couldn't have contemplated it unless there were immense levels of trust and understanding between us. The feelings were only going to be between him and me!

After looking at a lot of pictures and details I finally chose a guy who seemed more mature than the others. No tattoos. And I didn't want the 'toy-boy' kind of guy.

'It says he's nearly two metres tall,' James said nervously. 'And he looks very strong...'

I could see that he was worried what might happen if things didn't turn out well. What if the guy got carried away and James wasn't able to stop him fucking me without my consent? Would he be able to get him out of the house? I could see he was summoning up his courage to control all his fears.

We were going round and round the subject, savouring every morsel, trying to pluck up the nerve, until I decided it was time to make a decision. I put down my glass of wine and stood up.

'Okay, so make the call,' I said, 'and if anything bothers you, we stop it all.' I kissed him gently on his gorgeous lips before disappearing off to the bedroom to change.

James called the agency and explained what we were looking for. I gave a lot of thought to how I wanted to be dressed for this new experience as I listened to his voice on the phone in the other room. He opened the door, poked his head through and asked one last time.

'Are you sure you want to do this?'

'Yes, I'm sure.'

He went back out to confirm the booking and I went back to my wardrobe. Eventually, after trying a lot of different combinations, I selected a sexy wrap-around dress that you can just peel off by pulling one string in the middle, put a black bra and G-string and a black garter belt underneath. I lit some scented candles around the room and lay down on the bed. I could hear James pacing around the salon, waiting for 'room service' to arrive.

The time seemed to go very slowly as we waited, me in the bedroom and James in the living room, constantly questioning the entire process.

'I felt so alone,' he told me later, 'but so excited. I was determined not to show fear. I knew I had to be in control of this entire situation from start to finish.'

I blindfolded myself with a pair of black tights so that I wouldn't see the guy when he came in. This was anonymous sex we were buying, I didn't need or wish to meet him and make any conversation. That was not what he was there for. His personality was of no interest to me, only his tongue, fingers and penis – a living extension of our own bodies because we only have so many options with just two bodies. I lay on my back, my heart thumping in nervous anticipation. I heard the doorbell and there were muffled voices as the two men talked in the hallway. It seemed strange to hear another man's voice, a stranger inside my home.

'When the guy finally arrived,' James told me afterwards, 'I shook his hand as hard as I could to show him I had strength (even though I knew it would not change much). I stared him down, and right away took the initiative to pay him, to sit him down, and show him who was in control. We chatted for ten minutes, and I gave him the guidelines of what was okay and what was not. I told him we were here to play, there should be no kissing, no anal, that he should start with licking and see what developed. I told him that it was our first time. Then I just stood up and said: 'Okay, let's go. Follow me!'

The bedroom door opened and I heard their footsteps but couldn't discern which was which. No one was talking any more, just the sound of breathing. I felt like prey, pegged out on the bed, with two males closing in. Hands fondled my breasts, making me jump, and then someone was lying beside me, holding my hand and French kissing me deeply, so I knew that was James.

He must have motioned for the other guy to go to the end of the bed and gently remove my black Louboutins – the ones James calls my 'Fuck-me pumps'.

'The guy was so tall,' James told me, 'that when he kneeled at the end of the bed he was still about my height.'

I felt fingers lifting the folds of my dress apart, opening up the material and sliding my G-string down. I lifted my ass to make their removal smoother for him. James's lips were still on mine, our tongues entwined and his hands were cupping my breasts inside my bra, as two other big hands gently parted my thighs and I felt the warmth of another tongue exploring my thighs and calves and then the edges of my pussy, travelling over the most sensitive spots, venturing further inside, making me moan. I knew that I could make the sensation stop in a second if I just whispered to James that I was not happy, but I did not want it to stop. I wanted it to increase. I squeezed his hand tightly. The adrenalin in my system was speeding everything up and I felt breathless with excitement, not knowing what would happen next.

James knows me so well he would have been able to tell just from my breathing whether I was enjoying what was happening. He would have been immediately aware if anything was wrong or disagreeable for me and would react immediately. I also know him well enough to know that he was so excited at that stage he was almost coming and was having to keep himself under a tight rein to stop it happening too soon.

James stopped French kissing me and started to massage my stomach and breasts, so his hands were just centimetres away from this guy's face as he was licking my soft, shaved pussy. I could tell that the unfamiliarity of the situation was exciting him just as much as me. I could feel his pulse pounding the blood along every vein as we entered this new territory together.

Between my own moans of pleasure I could hear the sounds of the guy's tongue, lapping my wetness. After at least five minutes he stood up and started to get undressed and James moved in to lick me himself. I could feel his tongue, lips and breath.

'When he slid down his pants,' James told me afterwards, 'I was shocked by how well endowed he was – like in a porn movie – and he was hard as hell. My thoughts were oh my God – will she be able to take this? He knelt on the bed to your left, caressing his manhood, making it grow even bigger.'

Lifting my hand the guy placed it on his enormous erection. I gave a little start at the dimensions of it, turning my head in the direction where I thought James was so he could see my expression of amazement. The guy put his penis gently over my mouth. It nearly covered my whole face. I opened my lips and started tasting him.

James knelt on my right and gave me his dick too. I was alternately sucking both of them while the guy was fingering and caressing my pussy with his enormous fingers and James was fondling my breasts.

'It was so exciting to see your beautiful face so close between two dicks,' James told me later. He came very quickly after that.

Our guest then climbed onto the bed behind me, placed his hands around my hips and lifted my buttocks up so that he could enter me, doggy style. As his huge erection penetrated me James was kissing me passionately and holding me tightly as the guy behind began to move faster and faster, bringing me to a climax within seconds. I was tickling myself like a maniac until I was finally exhausted.

James could see that I'd had enough and told him that the job was over. Only once he was out of the bedroom did I pull off the blindfold. It was no more than twenty minutes since he had rung the doorbell and I had no idea what he looked like. Once he was dressed and out of the bedroom, however, he was in no hurry to leave the flat. He would have been happy for us to sit down and have a glass of wine together but we didn't need him to be our friend. We both wanted him out now so that we could be alone together and we could cuddle and talk about how it had felt.

'He just blew his chances of being invited back,' James said as he came back into the room having finally seen him out.

'How come?'

'He was so humbled to have been asked to make love to such a beautiful woman he said that he would be happy to come back and do it for nothing.'

'Yeah, right, like that's going to happen.'

'That's what I told him.' James lay down beside me and took me in his arms, both of us dissolving into fits of giggles at the same time. It had been a very interesting evening.

Thinking about what had happened intensified our levels of excitement as we made love for weeks after that. James often used a dildo in my mouth while he was tasting me or taking me, and sometimes the other way round. Since we had been back together again we felt that we had discovered something about sexuality that many people in our positions are never lucky enough to find. We would find ourselves sitting with friends at dinner and sense the dullness and lack of sexual tension between them, remembering the same feelings from our own marriages. But if we so much as glanced at one another across the table our thoughts would be going all over the place because of how we felt about each other and because of the places we had been together and the fun we were having exploring the possibilities of life.

CHAPTER SIXTEEN

Hannah is growing up so fast. Blonde with green eyes, she has a cute face and you can see immediately that she is a nice person. She already understands how lucky she is to grow up in our environment and that she has advantages other children can only dream of. She always cares that her friends are happy and she has a kind of generosity of spirit that I find amazing for such a young girl. I never see jealousy in her or an envy of stuff other kids have. When she can't get what she wants or I say I can't afford something or plans have changed she always says, 'Okay, Mom, not a problem.'

I think that today I am seeing the positive outcome of having been somewhat strict and rigorous about her education in the beginning. I always had rules and I always stuck to them. It is totally normal to her to make her own bed on weekends, to put her dirty laundry in the laundry bag and put empty bottles into the garbage. Obviously we fight sometimes. She has a strong character and tries to get her own way. Of course there are difficult phases, but we are both growing. She grows up understanding me more and I grow up learning how to educate her and understand her.

Like every mother I had to learn how to be a parent and understand the process of making Hannah her own person. I don't want her to be me. I don't want her to be anything I would have liked to be. I certainly don't want her to be something she doesn't want to be. I put a lot of effort into her education, finding good schools, pushing her to be a good student. I don't need her to be an 'A star' student but I think that high-quality schooling is important as well as learning languages and being aware of what's going on in the world. I want her to understand that things are difficult out there and that she has to fight to succeed. Most of all I want her to be happy and to have a great relationship with someone.

I'm proud of the mutual respect she and I have. She knows who is mother and who is child. She respects my privacy as much as I respect hers. If I am going to ask her to knock at my door before entering, I should never barge into her room unannounced. I never lie or talk bullshit to her. I have always spoken the truth, even when it stings, and I don't consider her less smart because she is a kid. I give straight answers to all her questions and she pretty much speaks to me openly about anything. Already I speak to her honestly about divorce, explaining that if she finds herself unhappy with a man she should be able to move on and be independent. A woman must have the freedom to choose the life she wants.

I don't miss Hannah when she's away with her dad. As long as I know that she is happy and in good health and that she is enjoying her time, my mind is peaceful and I am happy for her. If I sense there is a problem I become the most worried mother in the world and when that happens James is the rock beside me, supporting me and giving me strength. He is the best ear when it comes to conversations about Hannah and we have a lot of them. He is proud of how I handle her and of the person she has become. The older she grows the more I enjoy motherhood because it is more interesting, despite the inevitable challenges of the teenage years that are approaching.

Despite all the stresses, expenses and worries of motherhood I wouldn't be the woman I am today without Hannah.

* * * * * *

Aaron has been James's best friend for many years. They've done business together and in the unhappy years of James's marriage they used to go around together a lot in the evenings with their respective wives. Aaron's first marriage had foundered at much the same time as James's, and when his second one started to go downhill as well he continued to hang out with us on his own whenever his wife was away or didn't want to socialise.

He and James have always been on the same wavelength. They never fall out about anything and I find Aaron just as easy, and just as much fun to be around as James does. I think both James and I had felt that something unspoken was growing between the three of us for a little while, although neither of us would have known how to put it into words. I did not have the slightest interest in Aaron as a man, only as James's friend, as an occasional extension of us as a couple.

It was a Sunday night when everything changed. James and I had been dining and talking, but not drinking. We were still very clear-headed. James knew that Aaron was alone at home and suggested that we should ring him and see if he would like us to pop round. His house is always open to us.

It was a warm summer evening and I was wearing a denim mini-skirt with a very sexy blouse. I was feeling good about myself. When we got there we opened a bottle of wine and the three of us got to talking about sex. Aaron was the only person we knew who we were completely relaxed with as a couple, able to talk about everything that we were experiencing. We would spend hours in his company, drinking, playing poker, Trivial Pursuit or 'truth or dare' together, laughing all the time.

That evening, as we talked I was aware that both men were looking at my legs in the mini-skirt and each time I crossed or uncrossed my thighs James was pointing out that I was wearing beautiful little white panties. I was enjoying being the centre of attention, enjoying the wine, the cigarettes and the talk, and responding to the comments with flirtatious looks. After an hour or so of talking, when we were all deeply mellowed by the wine, Aaron announced he was going to take a shower, saying he wanted to be ready for bed as he had a tough schedule the next day.

He left us alone in the salon to go downstairs. All the talk about sex had aroused us. I could see that James was very unsure what to do next, not certain how I would react if he started kissing me passionately, but I could tell that he wanted to make love then and there. If we started to have sex we would almost certainly be caught and he couldn't gauge how I would react to that. He certainly didn't want to risk having his advances rejected; no man likes that.

I was settled comfortably on the couch, happy to wait and see what developed next, watching him as he stood up. I could tell that his heart was beating extremely fast; I could also see that he was horny. It seemed almost as if he actually wanted to get caught by Aaron and I felt a mixture of curiosity and anxiety as to how things were going to develop. How would Aaron react if that happened? Would it put him in an uncomfortable position? I wasn't sure if he trusted me in quite the same way he trusted James. I felt my heartbeat speeding up too. It was exciting, not knowing what would happen next, like the start of a new adventure.

James knelt down in front of me and gently but firmly parted my legs, exposing my little G-string. The tension was electric. We were alone in the living room of a house that was not ours. Our friend was downstairs showering and we had no idea how long he would be and neither James nor I had any idea how far the other would be willing to go.

He moved in and kissed me deeply, our tongues entwining. We could both feel how desperately the other wanted them. I ran my fingers through his hair, cupping the back of his head and pressing it downwards, caressing him and moving him so that his mouth and tongue were in exactly the correct spot to create the right rhythm to really start me flowing. I know he loves it when I guide him, when I touch his hair. I know he loves the way I taste. He peeled my panties off and as he started licking hard I saw Aaron coming back up the stairs in a bathrobe. He was standing, watching, and that made us both even more excited, our stomachs aching with a mixture of fear and adrenalin. I closed my eyes, suddenly shy to have him see me so exposed, but excited at the same time.

We felt vulnerable as well because it could still potentially backfire. For a moment James lost his erection completely. He was panicking and I felt it. I calmed him, showing him I trusted him as Aaron walked round behind the couch and stood looking down at James licking me. He was getting a great view. He looked James straight in the eye and indicated that he wanted to touch my breasts, as if asking him for permission. James nodded and Aaron embraced me from behind, over the back of the couch, wrapping his arms around me, his warm breath on my neck giving me goosebumps. He cupped both my breasts in his hands and I shivered with super-excitement.

After a few minutes James started to use his fingers in my pussy, making me moan with pleasure. I now had four hands gently teasing my body, touching my nipples, James's finger and tongue deep inside me. His erection was now fully recovered and he couldn't wait any longer. He had to have me.

James stood up and Aaron stopped the fondling. None of us spoke and the atmosphere was thick with pure excitement and lust. James guided me into a kneeling position on the couch and slid my mini-skirt up so that it was no more than a denim belt around my belly, exposing my ass for the first time to Aaron. I felt a little shy again but they are both gentlemen so there was no awkward staring. James moved behind me, Aaron still behind the couch, watching as James guided his dick into me from behind. He then indicated for Aaron to sit on the couch by my head and to hold my arms while he took me from behind. Aaron then took his dick out from the bathrobe and I grabbed it hungrily.

'Seeing you holding another penis in front of me,' James told me later, 'while I was in your juices was *soo* sexy. That vision kept me horny for weeks.'

I took the tip of Aaron's dick in my mouth, licking it and swirling my tongue around in a way I knew would drive him nuts. As I swallowed it deeper and deeper I moved into a real rhythm and the harder James thrust from behind the harder and deeper I sucked. At one stage James had to cool down and withdrew, motioning Aaron to move so that I could take his dick in my mouth instead. As Aaron moved behind me with his hard-on James suddenly realised that he had no condom and signalled for him to go and get one. For thirty seconds we were alone again.

'Are you okay, my beauty?' James whispered in my ear.

'Oh my God,' I gasped, 'this is so sexy! I love you. Are you okay?'

He nodded and smiled and I went back to tasting him with passion, awaiting the dick that was now being prepared behind me. As Aaron shyly and gently entered me from behind James felt my fingers tightening on his dick and my breath quickening, my mouth now still on him. It was all so new and so hot. We could both hear my wetness as Aaron moved rhythmically in and out. James reached under my arched body and caressed my clit, feeling the wetness. It was driving me insane as the two men stared at each other in disbelief at how sexy and how beautiful this entire scene was, none of us talking, all of us on fire, all equally astonished by what was unfolding.

James knows that I would never have any interest in having an affair with Aaron. Whatever we did together he would never be more to me than a friend and an addition to our sexual activities together. The difference was that this time we were involving someone who we knew and liked rather than someone we were hiring by the hour, and that meant there was the potential complication of how this would impact on our relationship with him as a friend. This new cocktail of possibilities made the situation even more unpredictable and exciting. The deal had been wordlessly struck as James's best friend became a living, breathing sex toy. There would be no more talking and no more laughing and it would always be James who orchestrated everything that would happen between us, until I said I'd had enough. We instinctively knew that he would understand what the rules were and where the boundaries would lie.

We are always very careful about preserving the boundaries. I don't even have Aaron's phone number; he's James's close friend, not mine; that relationship cannot be messed with. James is the love of my life and I know that situation will never change. When we have afternoons like the one on the boat that I described at the beginning of this story, what turns James and me on is the fun aspect, and the possibility to try new things. Sometimes we want to play with toys, but mostly we just want to play with one another's bodies. Sometimes we want a man to add spice to our lovemaking, sometimes a woman, sometimes both, but mostly we just want to be alone together. Sometimes one or other of us wants to be a voyeur, sometimes in control, sometimes controlled. The one thing we do not want is monotony and the one thing we do want is fun.

* * * * * *

Every time we try something new, something that we previously found scary or puzzling, we break through another barrier. There is a gradual escalation, but we discuss every step and talk and laugh all the time, so each move is carefully considered before we make it, nothing is left unsaid between us. We want to understand each other's desires as completely as we understand our own and that means we're constantly finding out new things about one another, which is exciting and stimulating.

The most important things to us are trust and honesty. If someone fakes an orgasm, for instance, it will never lead to a healthy sexual relationship. I admit I faked a lot of orgasms in my previous relationships. There can be many reasons why it might seem the easiest and kindest option, but it is always wrong to fake anything with the person you plan to live with for the rest of your life and plan to have an exciting, evolving sexual relationship with.

It takes a lot of confidence and trust in each other to be able to say 'I can't come', but in a strong relationship it shouldn't be a problem at all. It might just be that the position you are making love in doesn't suit you, or you might be at a place in your cycle where you get less wet. Your head might not be relaxed a hundred per cent (it can happen to me if Hannah is sleeping in the other room and I am feeling a little tense that she might wake up and interrupt us). Any lingering stress from the day might mean that your head is not there, or the rhythm may not be right or the TV show you just switched off could still be playing in your head and you are wondering how Jack Bauer will get out of his latest mess in the next season.

Sex is not just about body parts and erogenous zones. It's so much to do with the brain. So much needs to be right in order to have good, quality sex and amazing orgasms. So it would be totally ridiculous to think everyone is always reaching successful climaxes every time they make love.

I didn't know men could fake it too until James told me that he had faked it many times with Cecilia (how happy I was to hear that news!). I didn't quite understand it at first but I was intrigued and asked more questions.

'Well,' he explained, 'a guy can fake noises and spasms as much as a woman can. And since one can't really feel the semen inside – unless you check it out afterwards in the bathroom, well, men can fake.'

When I thought about it, it seemed so sad and we swore to each other that there would never be any faking between us. It was a relief to think that I was not obliged to come in order to make James happy or anything like that. Sex wasn't about orgasms but about the acts of love themselves, with all the foreplay that might involve. Since we have been together I have never faked it with James and I don't think he has either. We don't have to because we don't make it 'the point'. We ask each other maybe why we didn't come and then we laugh or talk about it and nothing becomes awkward.

Faking it is lying and lying is betrayal. How can you have an evolving sex life if you lie? By faking you make it impossible for either of you to learn from the experience, impossible to teach one another what you need and what you want and how you want it. It puts an end to open, honest communication. If your partner is tasting you, for instance, and you feel his tongue is just a centimetre away from a point where you would actually go crazy, but you just lie there and pretend because you didn't tell him to move his tongue a little, that would be so sad.

I am so lucky because we have this open conversation about my body and how I feel. James follows my body's cycles and how I evolve as a woman. He is alert and understanding and it is awesome that I can live so fully and freely as a result. A woman's anatomy is a complicated thing and he never stops wanting to find out more about every inch of my body, trying to discover how I might enjoy sex more or reach even better orgasms, and always with a twinkle in his eye and that cheeky smile playing on the corners of his lips.

At least once a week he will ask me by text or email, or face to face, 'Did you tickle today?' If I answer 'no' his next question is 'Why not?' If I answer 'yes' he'll want me to share the experience, telling him everything I was thinking about while I did it and my last thought before coming.

'I want to understand everything about you,' he says, 'your thoughts, your desires, your levels of horniness. I want to be inside your head.'

I find it very cool that I can share my tickling habits with him without any feelings of shame. I don't think that many people are able to do that. We were having dinner with a couple we know well recently when the wife suddenly announced that she had caught her husband masturbating over some porn on the computer, which had led to a big scene between them. She obviously wanted to embarrass him in front of us.

'You'll never guess what I caught John doing...'

It certainly embarrassed us because we could see how uncomfortable he was, but I don't think she got the reaction she was expecting. I simply couldn't understand why she would feel jealous of him touching himself. She seemed to feel threatened that he was pleasuring himself instead of screwing her, but to me it seemed these were two completely different things. They are complimentary things and both completely natural. James can touch himself in front of me if he wants, or even come on me, it's not a threat.

'How would you react if you caught James doing that?' she asked.

'You should have joined in,' I laughed, 'and had some fun together. We would.'

'Is that true?' she looked at James, unsure if I was teasing her.

'Of course it's true.' James wasn't about to start lying. 'Sometimes we watch porn together. Don't you? If I find a sexy scene that I think Penny will like I'll show her right away.'

She was obviously shocked that we were so open and free about such things and began to see that it might be her attitude that was the problem.

We talked a lot about the conversation after they had gone and we decided that the fact that she was shocked to find her husband did such things underlined our basic belief that every couple should communicate all the time. They should feel free to talk about their wildest fantasies without fear of shame, embarrassment or judgement. They should not have secrets and thoughts that they are ashamed to tell one another.

The ultimate for me when I am with James and Aaron is to be doubly penetrated, with one of them in my pussy while the other one is in my ass. James says it's sexy for them too because the wall between the two is thin and they can each feel the other one's dick inside me, both of them moving at the same time. I'm like a sandwich between them, one of them lying on his back with me straddling him so that I can then lean forward and let the other one into my ass. If it is James who is underneath then he and I can French kiss or he can lick my breasts while we fuck. I can whisper in his ear to tell him what is happening as Aaron enters me from behind, filling me up. If it is Aaron who is underneath I have to turn away because I have no wish to kiss him, and that slight awkwardness can heighten the feeling of strangeness and potential danger, becoming aroused in a different way as James enters me from behind.

CHAPTER SEVENTEEN

James is a complete voyeur and I love it. I love it that the moment I step out of bed in the morning I know he is staring at my ass. If there is a button open on my shirt he'll be staring at my breasts. When I'm stirring my drink he is gazing at my fingers. When I am in a store, trying on the simplest pair of jeans, he will be peeking through the curtains. When we have a massage together he is looking at the masseur's hands as they work on me all the time. Oh yes, my James is a huge voyeur.

'I'd really love someone to take proper professional pictures of you,' he said, 'all mine are so terrible.'

We were leaving a swingers' club in a castle in St Tropez, our spirits warmed with wine and he had picked up the card of a local photographer who was advertising that he specialised in sexy and nude pictures.

It was true what he said about his own photography skills, although we always had a lot of fun taking them. Once we got back to the hotel he showed me the guy's website and the pictures were really amazing, like '*La Dolce Vita* meets Helmut Newton', very sexy. We own a lot of erotic photography, as well as other erotic pictures and I liked the idea of having this guy turn his camera on me, especially if James was going to be watching it happen. I thought it would probably turn both of us on at the same time. James made the call and invited the guy to meet us at Nikki Beach for lunch the next day. The guy was an Australian and a bit of a hippy, but I felt very comfortable with him.

Once I had decided that I liked him we booked him for an entire day, during which he papped me like a celebrity, taking me everywhere from our bedroom to the beach and around the hotel corridors. It was really hot to have another man watching me so intensely through the lens, telling me what to do, where to look, what parts of my body to show to the camera, while all the time knowing that James and I were really the ones in charge of everything that happened. It was like playing the role of a film star or supermodel for real. People surreptitiously watched the beach shots from behind bushes, as if embarrassed by their own desires to stare and dream and speculate who I might be; actress or model, pop singer or porn star, someone important or someone notorious? And James got to be the voyeur watching other voyeurs watching me 'flashing' – so sexy.

Inside my head I was all these things without having to have any of the boring bits that come with the jobs. I was changing my outfits, sometimes wearing something sophisticated, sometimes flashing a breast or a buttock, sometimes leaving nothing to the imagination. James couldn't take his eyes off me, staying silent as he enjoyed the show, committing it to memory like a human movie camera. I loved every minute of it but we had no idea how the pictures would turn out.

The photographer was in control of where to shoot and what to wear. We just went with the flow. The next day he came to meet us again on the beach and showed us the results before giving us the CD containing more than five hundred pictures. We were both totally turned on by what he had achieved. Some of the pictures looked like a sexually explicit *Vogue* fashion shoot, others were like the classiest of Andrew Blake porn shots. I know James still looks at those pictures more often than he admits to.

'You want to marry me now, don't you?' I teased James.

'Ah, quit bugging me, woman,' he said, not taking his eyes off the pictures.

The photographer was obviously excited by the results as well because he asked me to sign a waiver so that he could use the pictures on his website and put on an exhibition. I was never going to agree to anything like that. I might have enjoyed feeling like a celebrity for a day, but I certainly didn't want to become public property. The session and the resulting pictures were just to turn James and me on, no one else. They were for our private collection, something else to go into our memory bank as a couple, a record of yet another fun day that we had spent together.

I have always loved St Tropez, ever since I used to visit as a girl with my parents. James and I have a routine when we're there. We go down to the port in the early morning, before the crowds arrive, buying ourselves books and magazines. We sit having coffee and breakfast and watching the boats, then we go down to Nikki Beach at around twelve to read and take lunch and a few glasses of wine, after which we dance and have fun in the sun. Almost everyone on the beach is beautiful and wants to flaunt it. The party finishes at eight in the evening, which is when everyone goes on to restaurants and clubs, or back to their villas and hotels.

Whenever we fly abroad I take care of all the travel arrangements. James knows that I negotiate well and trusts me to get the best deals. There is always so much planning with Hannah and school and my clients and Frederic's moods, everything has to be planned like an army manoeuvre. When it comes to the night before a trip, with all the arrangements in place, we are like excited school kids on the last night of term; we can't sleep, we can't screw, we do nothing, just wait for the time to fly past.

I always pack the bags for both of us. Not a great challenge with James, just blue shirts, white boxer shorts, black socks, knee-high only, and his trademark brown suede shoes. He never even looks inside the bags till we get to the destination. When I forget something, which happens often, and leave him stranded in a strange city with no socks or underpants, he just laughs and kisses me, caressing my tits and showing me how much he loves me and how little he cares about the trivia of life.

It is always good to do things at different times to the rest of the world. We often go to popular clubs on Monday nights, when we know that there will be fewer people, and then we might be in bed early on a Saturday night. We do not partake of any of the communal experiences like Christmas. The best thing about Christmas is that all the city centres are quiet because everyone has locked themselves inside their homes with their families and we can walk anywhere without having to contend with crowds, and be alone to talk without interruption. We don't even bother with one another's birthdays because we're already spoiling each other every day of every year. We buy each other presents, create surprises, go to the best restaurants and the best hotels all the time. We would not want to ration ourselves to doing these things only on 'special occasions'. We want to treat every day as a special occasion.

* * * * * *

We are always in a state of preliminaries and I find that very exciting, even when I am not necessarily in the mood. They start from the moment we wake up in the morning, when James will slide his hand between my legs as he gives me a morning kiss. He sleeps on my right and so my left breast is always the one he caresses first.

As soon as he's left the house my phone will beep with a message: 'Did you tickle?'

'No.'

'Why not?'

'Come back and do it for me with your tongue.'

'Can't. See you for lunch, naughty girlie.'

A minute later my phone beeps again. 'Did you tickle?'

If ever either of us is feeling shy about talking about something we immediately use texting or email. It has often saved our blushes or avoided an unnecessary confrontation or one of us being left feeling dumb about something. But James also uses texting to get me aroused throughout the day. I know he loves doing that and it is a way of shaping fantasies for me that he might still be feeling too shy to talk about directly over lunch.

He is always telling me how much he misses me on the rare days we don't have lunch together. He spends his whole time texting me, thinking of me... and I love it. I think we must easily have ping-ponged two hundred texts a day over the last eight years, often just simple one-worders.

When James is being driven home he'll be wanting to know what the programme is for the evening. Neither of us ever knows what is going to happen. It could just be a sandwich with a nice discussion while listening to Adele or

The Smiths, or it could be a night in with a television series but whatever it is he will always have that cheeky look on his face, no matter how I am dressed. He has this way of looking at me, of touching me. I know he wants me to be happy and well, and knowing that makes me feel so good.

* * * * * *

One morning I had taken Hannah to school and was thinking about the day ahead as I let myself back into the house. It was only eight-fifteen so I thought James might still be there when I got back and the thought of being able to see him before he left for work made my heart lift with anticipation. I came into the hallway and called his name but there was no reply so I knew I was alone in the house and felt a moment of disappointment, consoling myself with the thought that I would be seeing him for lunch in a few hours.

I shut the door and tossed the keys onto the table. As I was walking down the corridor I was hit by the full weight of a man's body, knocking me to the floor. I was still wearing my pyjama trousers, having just pulled on a coat and Ugg boots to go out. My assailant ripped them down to my knees. Pinning me to the floor, he fucked me hard and the most shocking thing was that it was a huge turn on.

I like sometimes to be submissive to James, but his natural instincts are always to be gentle and protective of me. He has had to learn how to please me by occasionally being rougher than his natural inclinations would make him, but he is a willing pupil, always wanting to try something new if he knows that it pleases me. It is one of the many reasons why I love him so much. I like it when he's rough with me, but I know it's hard for him because I'm so much his 'princess'. He was taking me doggy style when I first told him to spank me. He was happy to oblige and delivered the lightest of taps to my buttock.

'Do it properly,' I panted. 'Smack me harder!'

He even finds it hard to talk dirty to me, but he's learning fast because we communicate about it. It's almost impossible for him to contemplate degrading me when all he wants to do is praise me and tell me how beautiful I am and how turned on he is by every single thing we do together. He knows I was treated rough by one or two of my ex-boyfriends and he doesn't want to be the same kind of guy as them, but at the same time he wants to fulfil every fantasy I have ever had and so he will keep on working at it, pushing his boundaries a little further every day. We still have so many fun and exciting things to try.

* * * * * *

I had been reading a book about a dominatrix and James and I had been talking about the subject. I read a lot of books, especially during the summer holidays, and we talk all the time about everything that piques our curiosity or sounds like fun. One year James suggested we should read the same book at the same time so that we could talk about it as we went along, but I read much faster than him so he got left behind.

'So,' he said, late one evening after we had been talking about the book and drinking for several hours, 'Do you think it would be fun to go to a dominatrix?'

'It would depend what she was like and what she does,' I said. 'Would it hurt?'

'I'm never going to let anyone hurt you,' he laughed. 'You know that!'

'Then we're going to be a bit of a challenge to a dominatrix.'

We both started giggling at the same time. We must have talked round and round the subject for at least twenty hours before we were ready to make a move. Then we found a few numbers and James called them, but he hung up each time because the women who answered sounded too fierce, both of us giggling like naughty schoolgirls.

During the summer we always take Friday afternoons off so that we can make lunch stretch on for as long as we want and it was when we were playing around with the phone after one of those lunches that James found a Brazilian woman who sounded like fun.

'Is she nice?' I asked.

'What do I know?' he laughed. 'She's a dominatrix. She sounded fine on the phone. Let's go and find out. We can always run away if she's too scary.'

I wasn't at all sure that this was going to work since neither of us likes to be bossed around by anyone, but I could see James was as curious about the whole thing as I was and we were willing to play along if it meant we would have an interesting experience. We had an address and we were unusually nervous all the way there, making silly jokes and laughing too much, trembling, our stomachs tight with that familiar tension. That feeling was exciting in itself. We were sharing another new adventure, taking another step forward together. The Sat-Nav guided us to a pleasant-looking house in a suburban area and the door was opened by a woman dressed in a latex outfit that showed off her cute ass.

Having no idea what to expect heightened the excitement for both of us as she led us upstairs to a waiting room, where three or four working girls were sitting around. These girls, we soon discovered, were her slaves.

'So,' she said once the business had been done, 'would you like to go down?'

We followed her downstairs, our hearts in our mouths as she led us into a basement dungeon, complete with prison walls and iron gates. There was a lot of stuff lying around the room; nappies for grown-ups, a gynaecological chair and at least a hundred different dildos, some of which were enormous. There was a Sybian, a vibrating saddle with a giant phallus rising up out of it. There were finger-sized condoms and a mask with a ball to force open the wearer's mouth, and another with a huge dildo attached. There was a metal bed, with a board across it where the victim's head and hands could be locked, like in medieval stocks, and a cage. Everything was fascinating and absolutely nothing in the collection was going to turn us on. It was so obvious that we were out of place but by now I wanted to know exactly what happened in dungeons like this.

James asked if we could smoke and she said no, but when I asked she agreed. Already I could see that she was going to be picking on him more than me. She and I were going to be allies, which I thought was funny and had great possibilities. She disappeared for a few minutes, leaving us to look around, returning with a bottle of wine and a bowl of potato chips. We sat on the bed and I was beginning to feel almost relaxed with her. She went out again and the next time she returned she was pulling along one of her slaves on a dog lead. The girl was walking on all fours, looking cowed and frightened of the horsewhip in her mistress's other hand.

'Say hi,' she ordered the slave. The girl obeyed and then served us the wine, with her gaze averted, before sitting obediently in the corner, her eyes wide like a dog expecting to be hit at any moment. She was cute-looking too.

'So,' the Brazilian said, 'what do you want?'

'We don't know,' I said.

'So why are you here?'

'We're curious and we want to experience new things.'

James had taken a few chips from the bowl and one fell on the floor. She stared at it for a moment.

'Pick it up,' she instructed him and for a second I thought he was going to be unable to stop himself from laughing and ruining the whole scene.

'Pick it up,' I said, enjoying getting into character.

'Tell him to pick it up with his mouth,' the Brazilian added.

'Pick it up with your mouth,' I said.

James, fighting the urge to laugh, crouched down to obey. The domina caught my eye and raised her hand for a high five. We smacked palms and grinned. Now we knew what we wanted to do. We were a team and James didn't know which way to look!

Picking up a handful of chips she sprinkled them onto the floor as he bent down and started to pick them up with his lips. At that point she brought the whip down hard on his ass, making him jump from the sting.

'Stand up,' she ordered, whipping him again, hard, and he stood up.

'Strip off your clothes,' she ordered both of us and then dressed me in a tight latex corset that she laced up at the back, leaving James naked and vulnerable.

'Put these on,' she ordered, handing him a flowery dress, a wig with braids and a large pair of women's shoes.

James obediently pulled on the dress, wig and shoes because he could see I was really enjoying myself. He looked like a transvestite version of Heidi. Then she grabbed his hair and pulled it down hard, shouting, 'Lick her!'

As James obeyed she shouted abuse at him. 'You're doing it like shit!'

'This is your boyfriend?' she asked me, her lip curling with obvious disdain. 'Does he always lick you like this, like shit?'

She took hold of his head and moved it aside roughly.

'This is how you have to lick her!' And she started to lick me while aggressively holding his head close so that he could watch. She was physically hurting him and I could see that he was fighting back the angry tears, like a little boy being punished by a sadistic teacher, but by then I didn't care because she was using her tongue so expertly on me.

'Between the pussy and the anus,' she told him, 'is as sensitive on her as it is on you. Remember that!'

'Yeah,' I snarled, getting deep into the role-playing. 'Teach him the right way to do it.'

Pulling back from us for a moment she picked up a belt with a huge, aggressive dildo standing proud from the leather, and buckled it round her waist.

'Turn around,' she ordered me, 'doggy style.'

I obeyed and she forced the dildo into me, fucking me hard, ordering me to suck James while she did it, all the time telling me I was shit at sucking, just like him. By this stage James was having difficulty maintaining his erection as well as containing his giggles. I could feel his belly shaking with suppressed laughter and his penis was going hopelessly soft in my mouth.

'You can't get hard?' she spat contemptuously. 'You're pathetic!'

We had so much fun that night that we went back again and this time the Brazilian tied James into the gynaecological chair, making me lick him while she prepared an electrical probe to ram up his ass.

'I swear,' he said when he saw her approaching and realised what she was planning, 'you are not going to touch me with that!' she hesitated for a second. 'I swear,' he said again, 'you are not going to touch me with that thing!'

'Just give him a little sample,' I grinned as James shot me a dirty look. She touched him as if wielding a fairy wand and he jumped so high we all burst out laughing at once. James and I started French kissing, taking no notice when she ordered us to stop, and then we were making love. At that point the domina gave up and returned upstairs, still laughing.

CHAPTER EIGHTEEN

James had had a fever for three days, on and off, with no sign that it was going to develop into flu. He was exhausted all the time and running a temperature. Having endured a lot of sickness in my family I have a medicine cabinet as well stocked as a small pharmacy.

'You're such a hypochondriac,' James says whenever he glimpses inside it.

'No, I'm not,' I protest. 'I don't invent illnesses; I'm just well armed in case.'

I gave him some pills for his fever. He protested that he was okay and I had to beg him to swallow them, like he was a little kid who I had to fight with to make him better. We had a few calm days and a bit of rest, which undoubtedly did us both good after all our parties and craziness. Sometimes we just need to say 'stop!' and force ourselves to stay in bed at night and sleep like normal people.

Three days later I felt James getting out of bed several times during the night.

'Are you all right?' I asked him, half asleep.

'I'm okay, Penny, go back to sleep.'

I assumed he was just having trouble sleeping but at eight the following morning I woke to find he was not in the bed again. Suddenly the bedroom door opened and he practically crawled in, clutching his stomach and unable to stop the tears coming to his eyes. I jumped out of bed and pulled him up, immediately grabbing a pair of jeans and a pullover for him.

'Quickly!' I said, 'I'm taking you to the hospital. Why have you waited so long to tell me you are dying of pain?'

'I didn't want to wake you. I didn't want to bother you.'

'Well, it'll bother me more if you end up dead, silly one.'

I brought the car to the front door so he didn't have to walk too far. He could no longer disguise the fact that the pain in his stomach was killing him and I forced myself not to show how worried I was. Once we got to the hospital I made a huge fuss to make sure we got help as quickly as possible. No one seemed to be moving with any urgency, perhaps because we hadn't arrived in an ambulance with all the sirens wailing.

They took James away to an examination room. Even if I had wanted to go in with him he would not have let me. We still have a shy side to our relationship and I knew he did not like me seeing him in pain or being examined by doctors. Even though we both know we are there for each other in any situation, if we can avoid seeing the ugly stuff we will. Maybe it's a reserve that lasts because we never had kids together. When you have witnessed a woman giving birth what else can shock you in the medical area? We don't have that particular bond so I guess we will always remain a little reserved with one another about certain things.

Twenty-five minutes later James was wheeled out on a bed and taken into another room to get prepped for an operation. I ran after him, walking beside the trolley.

'I've got a big ulcer,' he explained. 'I need to be operated on right away. My God, the pain!'

As I watched him twisting in agony it felt like his pain and my pain.

'Don't tell my parents or the kids,' he said. 'I don't need Cecilia coming here at all and I don't want to worry the kids.'

My knees felt like jelly and my stomach was churning. Once I had kissed him goodbye and watched him being wheeled through the doors, I knew I had time to go home and prepare him a bag, since the operation would last at least two hours.

It takes thirty minutes to get from the hospital to our home so I knew I was going to be putting in some mileage over the next few days, going back and forth. From the car I phoned our house doctor to tell her what was happening because James trusts her and I knew he would like her to come and check on him.

At home I packed him a bag and drove back as quickly as I could, only stopping to kiss Hannah hello as she came out from school for lunch. I told her quickly what had happened. She loves James and I knew she would worry, but she also knows we are rocks and we don't panic, so her day continued on its normal routine as she ran up with her girlfriend to grab her lunch.

When I arrived back at the hospital James was still in surgery. Every minute of waiting felt like a day. I went three times to ask what was going on but no one could give me an answer. Two hours later they told me he was in his room and I could go in. He looked awful, still dizzy from the anaesthesia, with tubes coming out of his veins and connecting to three different bags of liquid. The doctor checked on him two minutes later and assured me that he would be fine. They had repaired what needed to be repaired and he just needed to rest there for a week and start eating plain foods, avoiding spices in the future.

I went back and forth for a week, at least four times a day, trying to make him as comfortable as I could. I brought books and magazines and one night I brought Hannah over with McDonald's for her and me so we could keep him company as he ate his dinner. She wanted to see him for herself to make sure he was all right.

James managed to downplay everything to Cecilia and keep her away. The thought of her visiting obviously made him very nervous. I let him handle his family issues and visits by himself.

It was the first time we had been separated for so long since getting back together, and never had it been for such frightening reasons. I felt desperately lonely every time I left the hospital and very conscious that my life without James would be reduced to nothing. I could not imagine being able to live for even a minute if I lost him. It made both of us even more aware that we should live every day to the full, as if it's our last, and enjoy every minute because life is so short and so unpredictable.

When I picked him up at the end of the week in order to drive him home, and tucked him in bed to rest, I was the happiest and most relieved person in the world.

* * * * * *

A few weeks later James and I were forced by family responsibilities to be apart for a whole weekend. Sometimes I think that the bond we have with one another makes us like twins, giving us a connection that causes us actual physical pain when we are pulled apart. We feel we need to breathe the same air. We need to have all four of our eyes seeing the same things and the moment we are separated it starts to hurt. If one or other of us just leaves the room for an hour or two it feels like days. I don't think many people are lucky enough to experience a love this powerful, this unconditional. It is like the bond you might have with a child or a parent but with the huge physical attraction and sexual desire added.

On top of that, it was one of the worst weekends of my life. My father had called me to go down and help him with my mother, whose illness had taken a turn for the worse. Seeing this once proud, beautiful and intelligent woman reduced to a shadow of her former self broke my heart. I cried almost the whole weekend. My poor, frail father was struggling to look after her full time while his own health was on the verge of collapse.

James had taken his kids away for the weekend and was messaging me from McDonald's and any number of other places in desperation, wanting to be with me, wanting to help me, but at the same time wanting to be a good and attentive father too. On days like those it was hard to imagine that we were the same people as we were in our life together. It would have been so easy to give up the struggle of keeping our relationship alive and exciting when there were so many other emotional demands, but it actually made us even more determined never to give up on living life to the maximum whenever we could, whatever demands our family responsibilities might put on us.

At ten o'clock on the following Monday we were both back at work in Lugano, messaging each other and counting down the hours till we could be together again. James had been telling Aaron about our visits to the domina and Aaron now wanted to get whipped around a little himself. Apparently he craved a little bit of rough treatment. James decided to book a great restaurant for supper so we could relax and do what we enjoyed most, talking over the possibilities.

That evening, relieved to once more be free of the responsibility of being a nurse and daughter, I got dressed without really thinking. I was just looking forward to having a nice bottle of white wine and a relaxing dinner in order to wipe the whole horrible weekend from my mind. I heard Aaron arriving and when I went to join them both I found myself standing under their gaze in the middle of our salon in a short leather skirt, opaque tights, high heels and a grey sleeveless turtleneck. My hair was pulled back fiercely and I had applied smoky eye make-up. I hadn't planned the outfit, I just felt good like that.

'Wow!' both guys said at once, 'you look like a domina yourself.'

Two bottles of Chablis and two packs of cigarettes later we were driven back home from the restaurant and opened another bottle. After a while James started to provoke Aaron, telling him he wouldn't dare to go to our bedroom and allow himself to be smacked around by me. It took no more than three minutes before he had accepted the challenge and I had two men lying naked in my bed, waiting for me to do whatever I chose to them.

I strode into the room and ripped the duvet off them, not intending to give them anywhere to hide, waving the key to our 'adult toys drawer' in Aaron's face.

'I've had a bad weekend,' I hissed, hamming it up like our Brazilian friend. 'I am not in a pleasant mood.'

James knew I was acting, but Aaron didn't. He was laughing nervously, not sure what to do, which I could see was making James laugh too.

'Shh,' I hissed, putting my finger to my lips and staring at them till they both obeyed.

Opening the drawer I took my time selecting about ten dildos in a variety of shapes and sizes. One was a small white one of the sort that people used in the eighties. Two were glass. There was a big black one and another in a banana shape. I also took out a leather whip and black leather thongs, which I used to tie their hands above their heads. As I strapped on a leather belt with a dildo attached I could see from his eyes that Aaron was now apprehensive, no longer able to move should he decide he wanted to escape and unsure what my intentions might be towards him. Both of them now had erections.

I lined all the instruments up next to him, slowly and methodically wiping down each one in turn, threateningly close to his face. Once I'd finished I lifted the whip and slapped his dick sharply.

'That's a horrible little thing you have there between your legs,' I snarled.

He opened his mouth to reply but I slapped his face.

'Stay absolutely still,' I whispered into his ear, 'do not move a single muscle.'

I stalked to the other side of the bed, my expression giving away nothing, pulled my tights down a few inches so that they still held my legs close together and mounted James's erection through my crotch-less black panties as Aaron lay watching, helpless to do anything. I rode James like a horse for no more than ten seconds before lifting myself off and pulling my tights back up, leaving him simpering for more.

As I walked back to the other side of the bed our weak, pathetic little guest sniggered nervously, which earned him several strokes of the whip across his ass and a string of insults.

'Can I lick one of your tits?' he begged.

Without saying a word I pulled up my shirt, pushed my nipple into his face and let him have the pleasure for three seconds – enough.

I went back to James's side and sat on him again for a minute. He was fantastically aroused by everything that was going on, exactly as I intended him to be. I then rolled our defenceless friend onto his stomach and licked his cute ass, alternating each tasting with a sharp slap on his ass cheeks, making him moan and twitch with a mixture of excitement and pain.

'Now,' I announced aggressively, 'I'm going to stick my pink glass dildo up your ass.'

The excitement I had seen in his eyes now verged on panic but he didn't dare protest for fear of the sting of my whip.

'I'm going to fuck you hard,' I hissed threateningly in his ear.

I swiftly applied some lube before ramming the dildo into his ass, sending a spasm of shock and awe through his whole body, while James watched from the other side of the bed in a state of total excitement. I ripped off my top and pushed the dildo in deeper and deeper, all the way to the end, fucking him harder and faster. At the same time I leant over and tasted James, making him twist and squirm in ecstasy like a panic-stricken fish out of water. I then allowed him to take me from behind. I was still wearing the skirt and crotch-less knickers, with my tights only lowered a few inches, making everything extra tight.

James came inside me at the same moment as I saw Aaron coming from touching himself with his bound hands, the dildo still in his ass. I then made myself come by touching myself while both men sucked on my breasts.

I am close to forty years old. It was a Monday night, four o'clock in the morning, and I had two handsome men in my bed and a whip in my hand. How much better can life get than that?

It ended with all three of us on our hands and knees, searching the floor for used condoms, dildos and bottles of lube, getting the room clean and laughing uncontrollably. Three hours later Hannah came in to say good morning before going off to school. By eleven I was sitting in a client's office with a huge smile on my face, thinking, 'If you only knew what I did last night...'

I'm often saying that I don't want to 'die stupid' and sometimes when we've done something new, when we're driving home afterwards and I am relaxed and laughing, I will say, 'So, now I can die tomorrow, it's okay.' But I won't die for a long time yet because we still have a lot more things to try.

James and I know how lucky we are to have found each other. We are like two kids playing all the time, whether it is on a golf course, in a club or a restaurant or on a beach. We both enjoy our work and we are able to share everything we do with one another, always together, always talking and debating, enjoying a view or a good bottle of wine. We know just from looking around at the lives of all our friends how unusual it is to be able to live like this. At the same time we still have to deal with the daily chores of raising an extended family and balancing the books, but even there it is so much better when you are able to do it together, knowing your partner will support you no matter what decisions you make.

James says that he plans to continue living at a hundred and fifty miles an hour every day of his life until he is sixty, when he will go out with a bang. I have no intention of letting him go anywhere. Even if I had never met him before and passed him on the street I know he would still make my heart beat as fast as it did that day in the coffee shop, twenty-four years ago. Every time we have a date I still have butterflies in my stomach as I get close to the appointed time, even if it has only been a few hours since I last saw him. I always get antsy before he enters a room, even if we only parted a few hours before. I can't wait to feel him close and to smell his skin. If the day ever came when I couldn't smell his body any more I would wilt and dry up like a flower without water.

EPILOGUE

Later that day we were out on the golf course together and I was taking in deep breaths of fresh alpine air as James prepared for his shot, staring out across the lake to the mountains beyond. I could feel the warmth of the sun on my face as I closed my eyes and allowed my thoughts to wander. I felt like the luckiest woman in the world. Looking back over the previous twenty-five years I wondered if there was anything I could have done differently, anything that would have led to an even better outcome to our story.

People who know how in love we are sometimes ask whether we regret not having a child together. We have given the matter a lot of thought, discussed it for hours, and I am sure that if I had borne a child for James our relationship would not be the same as it is now. It's a wonderful, romantic idea but the reality of childbirth and parenthood is very different to the dream.

I know from experience that the moment a couple gives birth, their relationship changes. You were two in the beginning; intimate, private, focused totally on each other. Suddenly another tiny human being arrives and messes up your entire household. Sleepless nights make you nervous and aggressive. Motherhood turns you into a bitch, certain that the guy who was previously the centre of your life is not even capable of taking care of *your* child. You have no more time to have sex and frankly how exciting is it to screw amidst the aroma of diapers and with breast milk stains on the duvet because you are totally convinced that breastfeeding has to be done in your own bed? (I don't believe that, by the way.)

In the romantic lead up to the birth you were probably sure you wanted your husband to be present and maybe even film the whole process. The sexy little pussy he had desired and tasted before is stretched and contorted before his horrified eyes into a swollen, monstrous thing with a blood-smeared head popping out. If he's lucky he'll also witness the doctor cutting it open and sewing it together again afterwards. Is that image ever going to be exciting for future sex? I can't blame men for losing their desire for their wives after those visions. From that moment on she has become something else; the mother of their child. That's what we turn into and not surprisingly we feel ashamed of this feeling. Nobody admits it, but it's normal.

From the moment of birth onwards everything is about the baby and the couple is not the focus any more. Just look at them in the streets with their families, none of them saying what they are thinking because of the toddlers looking up at them with wide eyes, apparently taking in every word. They all look exhausted, the men pushing the strollers in front of them, staring into space and thinking, 'What am I doing here?'

If James and I had been through that experience together I don't believe we would have come out of it desiring each other so passionately. As a couple we would have drifted apart, allowed to do so because we have that human being tying us together forever. One of the benefits of being divorced parents is that every second weekend and half of our vacation we are without kids and can live like teenagers ourselves. That would not be the case if we were parents together. As much as our love is strong, it would not have stayed the same way it is today.

I can't say that we would not be together but we would certainly not have the same relationship of utmost respect towards each other. I like that James is a dad, I think parenthood has made him an even better man, but it wouldn't have been the same.

It is impossible to overstate the value of sharing your life with someone you are totally at ease with, someone you can talk to about every thought, fantasy or vision that might cross your mind. There are still a million things inside my head that I would like to share with James and I know he is the same. There may be subjects we are both still shy about saying aloud, but we know that when we do, whatever we say will never cause a problem.

Opening my eyes again and staring out at the perfect view I wonder if our relationship would have been the same if we both had to work long hours at jobs we hated just to earn a minimum wage. I know we've been lucky with money, but it's still a question of mentality and character. I have never ever thought, 'I won't go out tonight because I have a hard day at work tomorrow.' Even in all my previous jobs I could stay out late or watch movies until five in the morning and still be fresh at work at eight. Maybe it's a leftover from my youth when my father would say, 'If you can dance until five in the morning, then you can also get up and work.' I've always wanted to have both and James is the same. We are lucky that we both want the same things from life.

If we didn't have money it would make no difference. We are self-sufficient and I would have as much fun as I have today however much we earned. Money is not an issue for the fun. I could dress in cheap clothes and still make them look sexy. Caviar is a thrill but I love McDonald's just as much and cheap wine makes me drunk in the same funny way. Frankly, if we didn't have all the kids, a small flat would be perfect. I don't care about cars and I wouldn't die without my Rolex or my pearls.

All these things are a bonus and very, very much appreciated but I would trade them all for just one day of being with James if that was the choice, and it would not detract from any of the fun. When we first met in school we drank cheap beer and ate pizzas and oh my God, did we have fun. We are still the same people, just older and smarter.

So, what will I do if Hannah comes to me in ten years' time and tells me she is in love with a man who can't marry her? I will not be able to tell her to wait because nobody knows if that person will ever go back to her or if there will be a happy ending. No one should spend their whole life waiting. I guess I would advise her to have faith and to be patient. And I would convince her that she should never doubt herself and that if that person truly loves her, somehow it will work out. I would also advise her not to rush into other relationships in an attempt to compensate for what she has lost, that's never going to be a solution. I would advise her to be truly honest with herself and to listen to her heart.

I would have loved being with James in the years when he made his first career steps. I would have enjoyed boosting his confidence rather than pulling him down and trying to undermine him, but if we had been together through those early years I don't believe that we would have evolved sexually in the same smart, adult way.

If we could go on like this until we die that would be perfect. I want us to continue exploring life, living out our deepest fantasies and sharing. Share, share and share. I want to climb up the stairs with him and grow more and more. I want to be able to build even more of a past with him.

Meeting him that day in the coffee shop made my life and I am thankful for every part of the experience. All the waiting and all the pain were worth it. If we could die the same day and be buried next to each other that would be the best end because I couldn't bear one day without him in my life.

'Are you going to take this shot or not?'

His voice snaps me out of my reverie and I see him standing in front of me with his hands on his hips. Even with the sun in my eyes I can see he is grinning and looking at me in that sexy way of his. It's almost as if he was reading my mind.